BREXIT

A DRAWN-OUT PROCESS

ART.50
SUNLIT UPLANDS
MAP
DOVER
6 TESTS

CARTOONS BY JAMES MELLOR

AUTHOR OF DRAWN FROM HISTORY

Published by

Filament Publishing Ltd

16 Croydon Road, Beddington, Croydon,

Surrey, CR0 4PA, United Kingdom.

www.filamentpublishing.com

Telephone: +44 (0)20 8688 2598

© 2019 James Mellor

ISBN 978-1-913192-61-7

Printed by 4edge Ltd.

The right of James Mellor to be identified as the author and illustrator of this work has been asserted by him in accordance with the Designs and Copyright Act 1988.

All rights reserved.

No portion of this book may be copied in any way without the prior written permission of the publishers.

What people are saying about James Mellor's *Drawn From History*

I love this book; bringing history to life through cartoons is genius.
Gregg Wallace - Host of BBC's Time Commanders and Masterchef

A Great book that will have you laughing out loud as you browse dozens of splendidly witty cartoons.
This England Magazine

A hysterical history of a nation's finest, and not so finest hours.
The Reigatian

His work simultaneously pokes fun at the past whilst celebrating it and provides an entertaining opportunity for readers to engage with history.
OVL Magazine

½ PRICE COLANDERS

Agincourt Entrepreneur

DRAWN FROM HISTORY
A Cartoon Journey Through Britain's Past

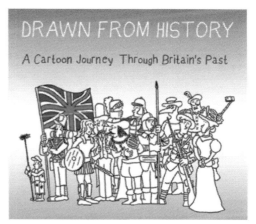

NOW ON SALE

Acknowledgements

I would very much like to thank:

The incompetent and ridiculous politicians inhabiting Westminster and Brussels, without whom this book would not exist or would be far less amusing.

The Professional Cartoonists' Organisation and the Cartoonists' Club of Great Britain for the warm welcomes they have given me and the professional support they provide.

Lee Robertson for not only writing the foreword to this book but for allowing me an amazing degree of creative freedom to draw for Octo Members Group.

All the clients of JMC, who have either seen the potential cartoons have for communication or have been willing to trust me, take a punt and see what happens.

The Guild of Entrepreneurs in the City of London for your support in my career and for allowing me to indulge my passion for history in an official capacity.

Tallie, for making life such fun and being an endless source of hope.

Eli, who ensured his early arrival didn't disrupt the creation of this book too much.

My wonderful wife Rachel for her unceasing support, optimism, and love. Nothing I have achieved in my cartooning career has been without your help.

Hera the cat, I suppose. Though she continues to provide no actual help whatsoever.

About the Author

James Mellor is a freelance cartoonist based in the UK. He is a member of the Professional Cartoonists' Organisation and the Cartoonists' Club of Great Britain.

His cartoons have featured in numerous publications, including *Private Eye*, *The Sunday Telegraph* and *Business Impact*, and have been exhibited at *House of Fraser* (2018), *Art 4 Africa* (2018), *Herne Bay Cartoon Festival* (2018 & 19) and *The London Cartoon Show* (2019).

To put cartoons to use in the corporate world, James launched James Mellor Creative in 2012. JMC helps people and businesses turn their ideas into usable, engaging and memorable content and is built around his three areas of expertise: cartoon illustrations, research and writing. In this capacity, he has provided words and pictures in newsletters, conferences, websites, blogs, and social media posts for large multinationals, individuals just starting up, and many businesses in between.

A History graduate from the University of York, James is the author/illustrator of *Drawn From History: A cartoon journey through Britain's past*, *Drawn from 2017*, *Great Entrepreneurs From History* and is the Honorary Historian to The Guild of Entrepreneurs in the City of London.

James lives in Rushden with his wife Rachel, daughter Talitha, son Elias, and a small, sociopathic cat.

Foreword

It takes a rare talent to be able to make some sense of a subject as fraught and divisive as Brexit let alone be able to draw insightful, witty and thought-provoking cartoons on the subject. I believe this book does this in abundance and that you will, despite the seriousness of the situation, find much to amuse you. It is this gift, drawing on the noble tradition of political satirical cartoonists, that led me to commission James for a unique weekly cartoon for the Octo Members Group.

Lee Robertson BA FRSA Chartered FCSI
CEO
Octo Members Group

Table of Contents

Introduction

The important thing to remember about Brexit is that no one comes out of it well. Not the ardent Brexiteers with their bizarre Blitz spirit and unicorns. Not the hard line Remainers with their hysteria and hypocrisy. Not the fence-sitters, who block any way out of the mess in either direction. Not the European Union, whose intransigence has reinforced the negative perceptions that led us here. There are no Brexit heroes. On the plus side, it is a situation ripe for cartooning.

You may have heard this once or twice on the news, but apparently Brexit is a divisive issue. Just to discuss it (or heaven forbid, publish a book of cartoons about it) only makes it worse. Sorry about that. However, this book isn't about taking sides. Michael de Adder was writing about cartooning US politics, but the sentiment of his comment can be applied equally well to Leave and Remain:

"We're not Democrat or Republican, we're just anti-stupid. We attack both sides. We just want to illustrate the stupidity."

Yes, those in the driving seat receive more attention in this book, but that's to be expected as they're the ones with the power. However, the supporting cast are equally treated with ridicule. I've added a few notes where I've thought necessary to jog memories but hopefully the events depicted will come flooding back with horrible clarity, like an undercooked meal of EU horse meat or American chlorinated chicken.

On that note, I should conclude by thanking you for buying this book, expressing my hope that you enjoy the cartoons, and politely depart. I'd be happy if you stopped reading here and dived into the pictures as the next sentence may make you go off me.

Brexit has been rather good for me. Awful as it may be, this mess has helped to once again demonstrate the power and utility of cartoons. The Brexit process is two things if nothing else: It is complicated, and it is often funny. Cartoons use humour to help people understand and care about complicated situations. They cut through the waffle to mock those who hold responsibility. When times are difficult, they cheer us up. These have been good years for drawing cartoons.

Politics has become as much of a water-cooler talking point as *Game of Thrones* or *Strictly Come Dancing*. There were many flaws with the 2016 referendum, but it has genuinely engaged people with how their country is governed. For me, cartoon commissions used to involve drawing jokes about a particular sector or industry. Increasingly I am asked to take on current affairs and news topics – that is what clients' customers or employees want to see in their newsletter, social media feed, or presentation.

Cartoons are in demand and that is a good thing for everyone. They educate and inform. They are a catharsis and a coping mechanism. In British culture we have always used humour and mockery to see us through times of great change. These past few years, we've needed to.

I hope you enjoy the cartoons.

James

Early Days

How young and innocent we were back in 2016. There's an unusual amount of optimism in these early Brexit cartoons, which is nice. There are also more than a few indicators that this simple binary referendum was going to descend into a Groundhog Day style waking nightmare in which we relive the same tedious arguments again and again. No one on any side ever actually gets what they want, yet to compromise becomes the greatest sin of all.

Do enjoy this pleasant stroll through happier times.

New Horizons.
New Challenges.

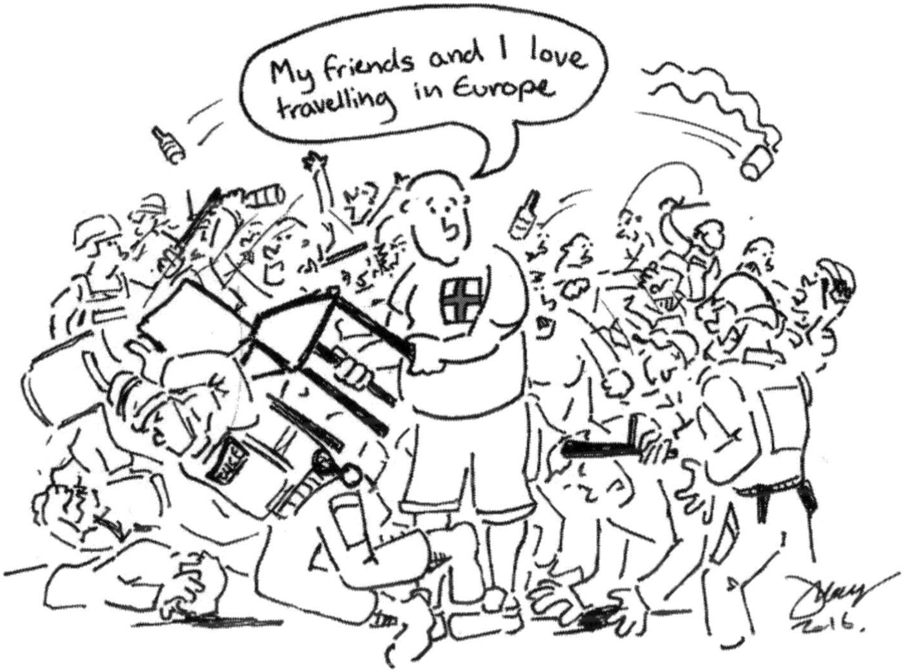
My friends and I love travelling in Europe

CHILLIN MEETIN TOURIN #VOTIN

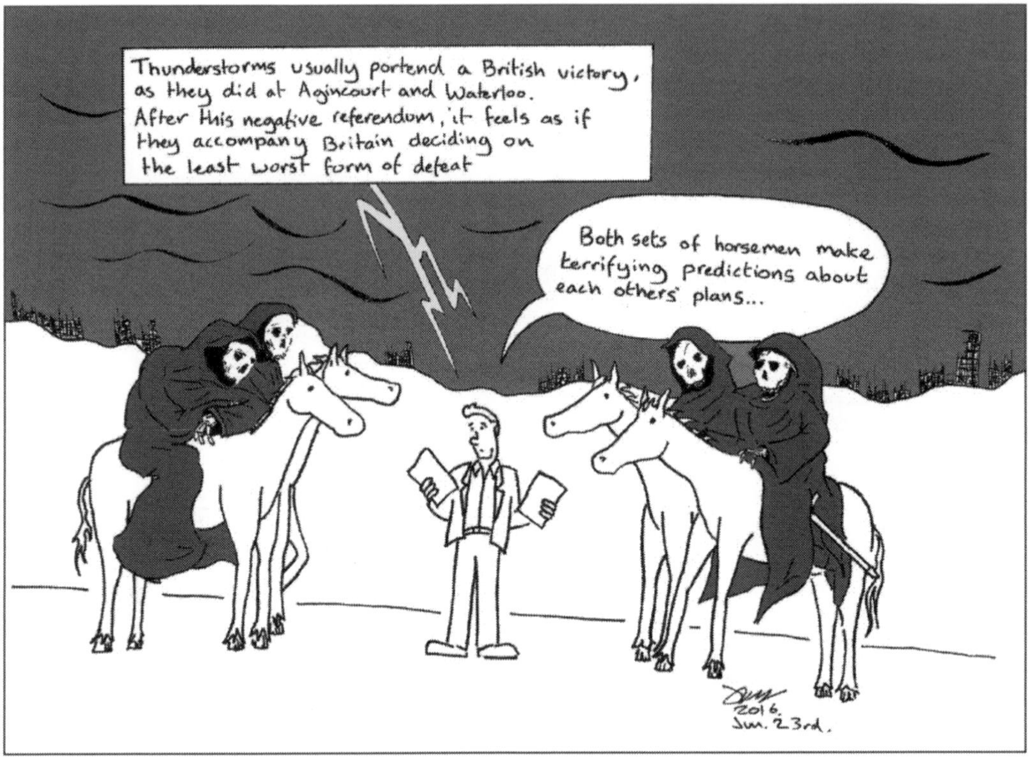
Thunderstorms usually portend a British victory, as they did at Agincourt and Waterloo. After this negative referendum, it feels as if they accompany Britain deciding on the least worst form of defeat
Both sets of horsemen make terrifying predictions about each others' plans...
2016. Jun. 23rd.

A sketch from the day of the Brexit referendum

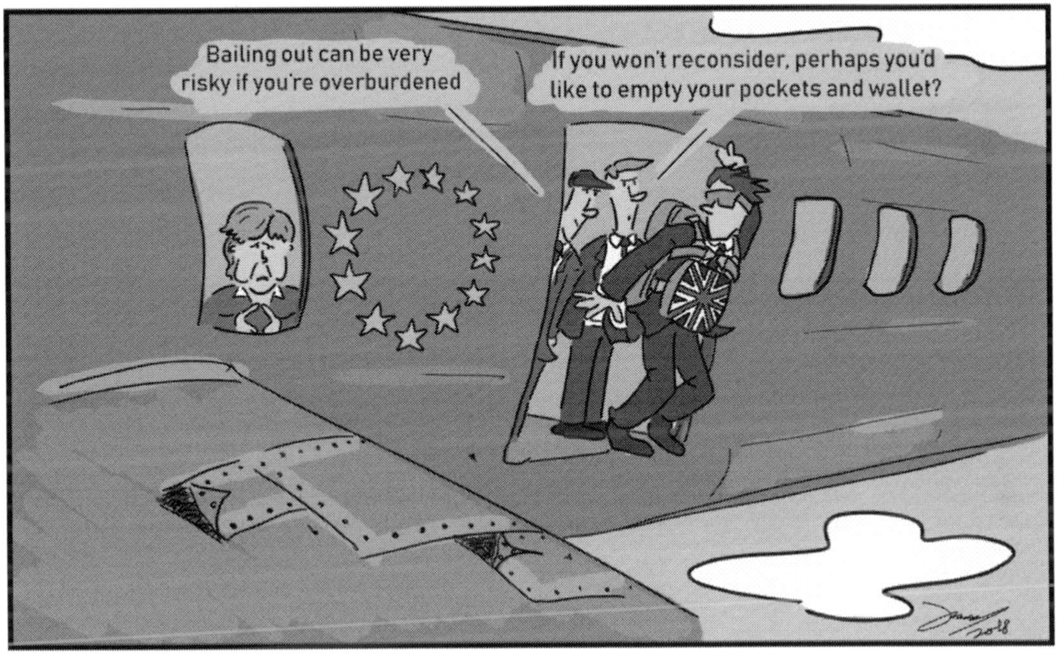
Bailing out can be very risky if you're overburdened
If you won't reconsider, perhaps you'd like to empty your pockets and wallet?

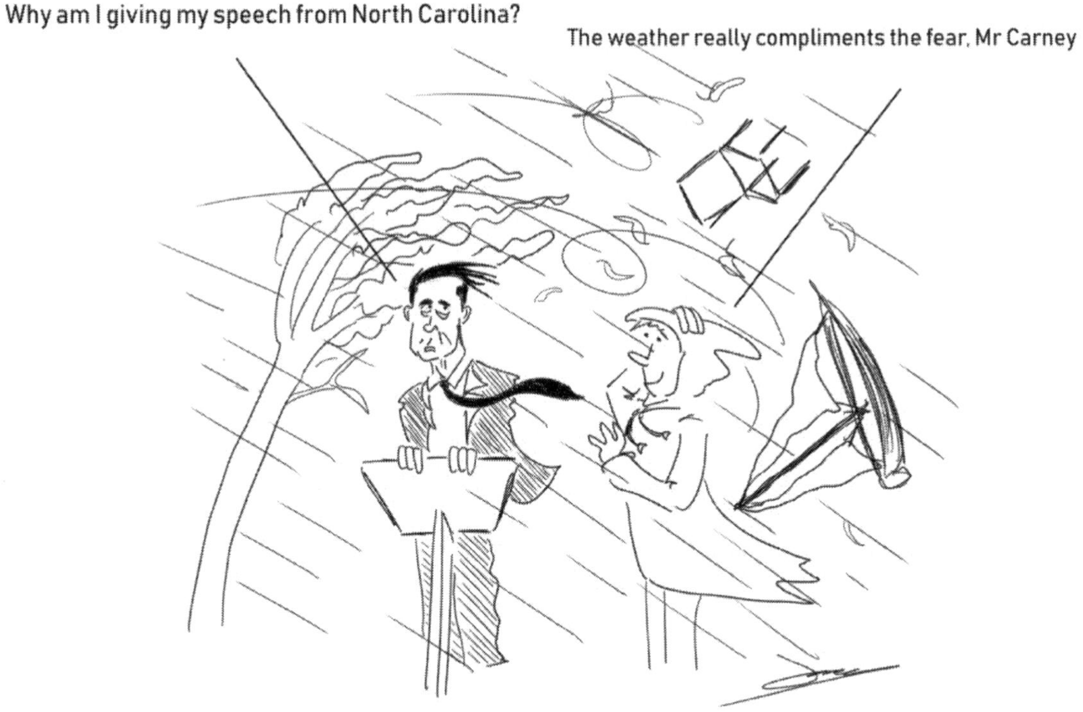
Why am I giving my speech from North Carolina?
The weather really compliments the fear, Mr Carney

Hurricane Matthew 2016

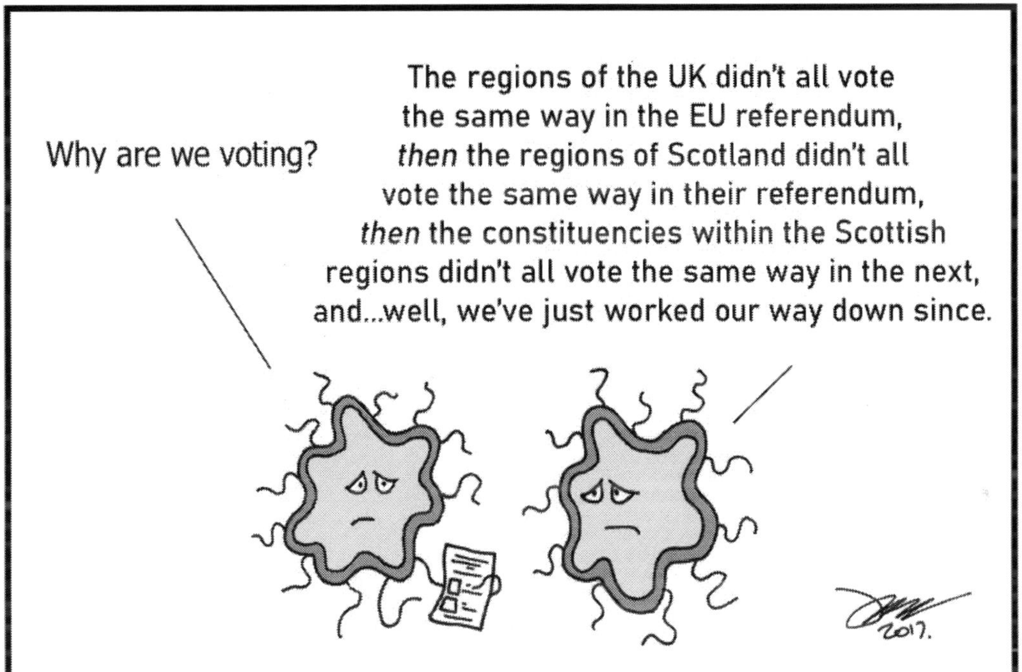
Why are we voting?
The regions of the UK didn't all vote the same way in the EU referendum, *then* the regions of Scotland didn't all vote the same way in their referendum, *then* the constituencies within the Scottish regions didn't all vote the same way in the next, and...well, we've just worked our way down since.
2017.

Bacterial Referendum 2056
(should the head or the heart get to cast the vote for this individual's body in the household vote on independence)

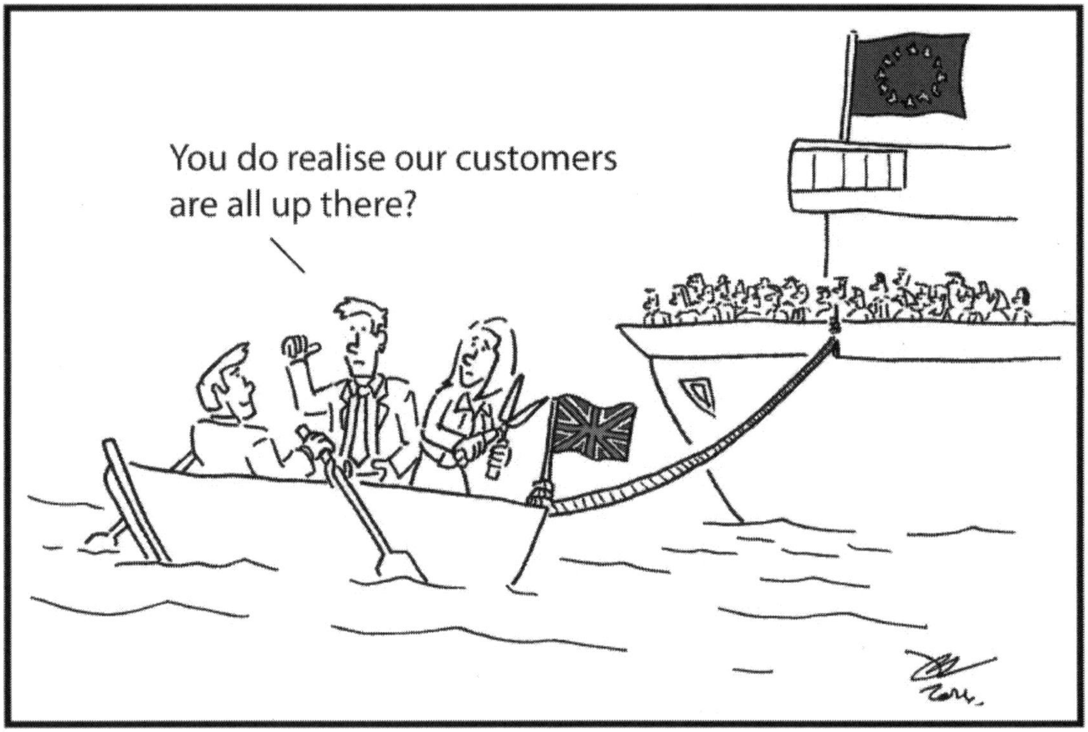
You do realise our customers are all up there?

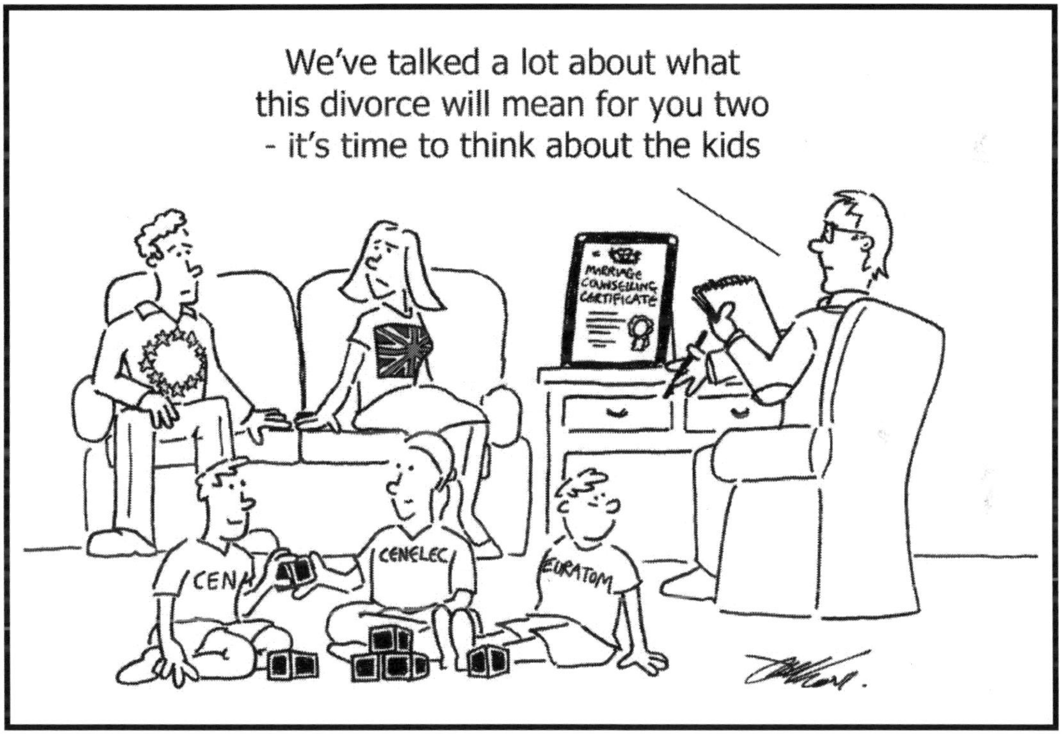
We've talked a lot about what
this divorce will mean for you two
- it's time to think about the kids
MARRIAGE COUNSELLING CERTIFICATE
CEN
CENELEC
EURATOM

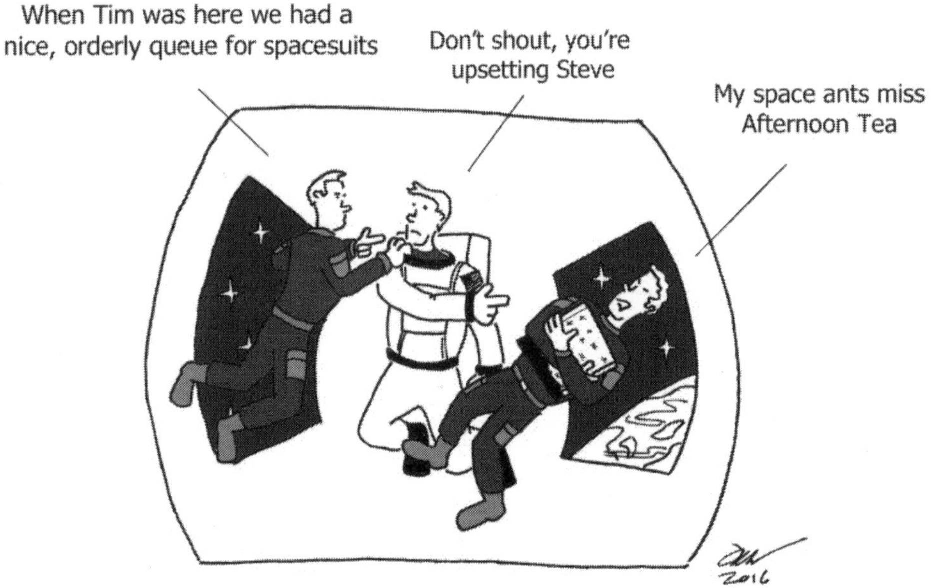
When Tim was here we had a nice, orderly queue for spacesuits
Don't shout, you're upsetting Steve
My space ants miss Afternoon Tea

Chaos following a 'Brexit'

Major Tim Peake leaves the International Space Station 2016

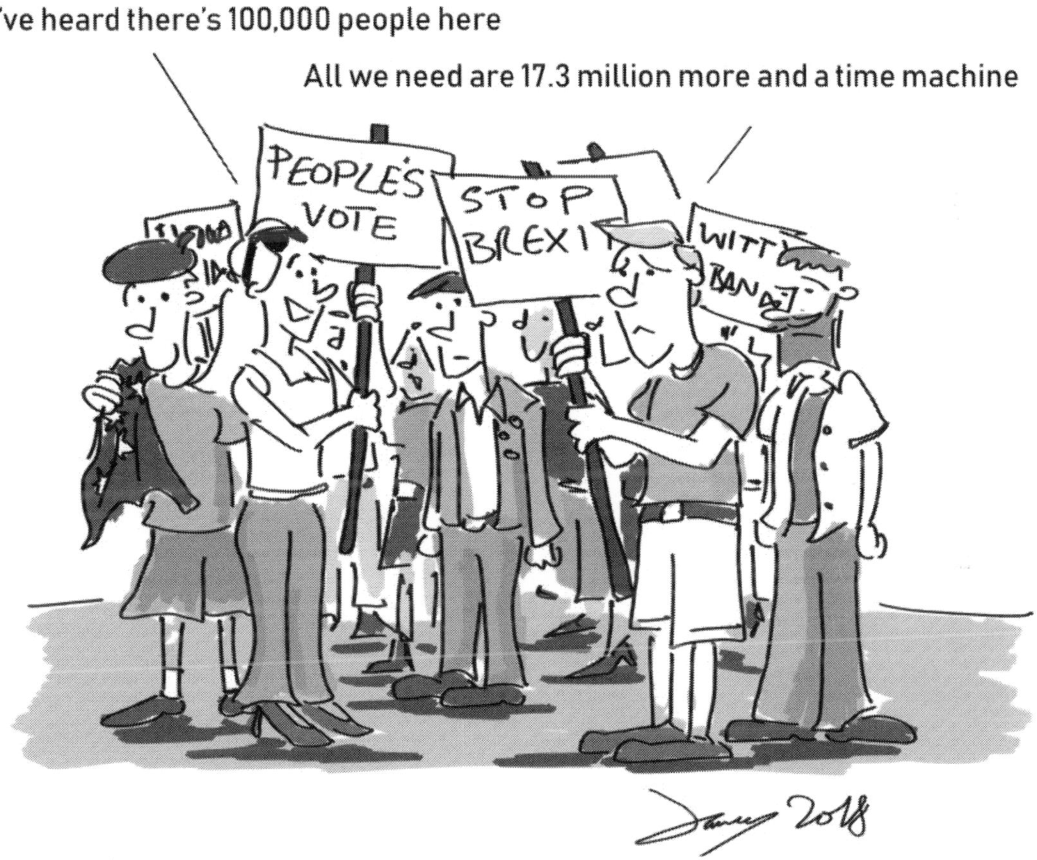
I've heard there's 100,000 people here
All we need are 17.3 million more and a time machine
PEOPLE'S VOTE
STOP BREXIT

Sealing a Deal

Contained within this chapter are cartoons that hopefully capture the beauty of *Brexit Negotiations* – that most wonderful of meetings between those who don't know what Brexit they want and those who don't understand how negotiations work. What could possibly go wrong?

You may note that time skips forward very rapidly during this period. This, as you may remember, is because very little progress seemed to be made. Not to worry, though. It's not as if triggering Article 50 had activated a ticking countdown or anything.

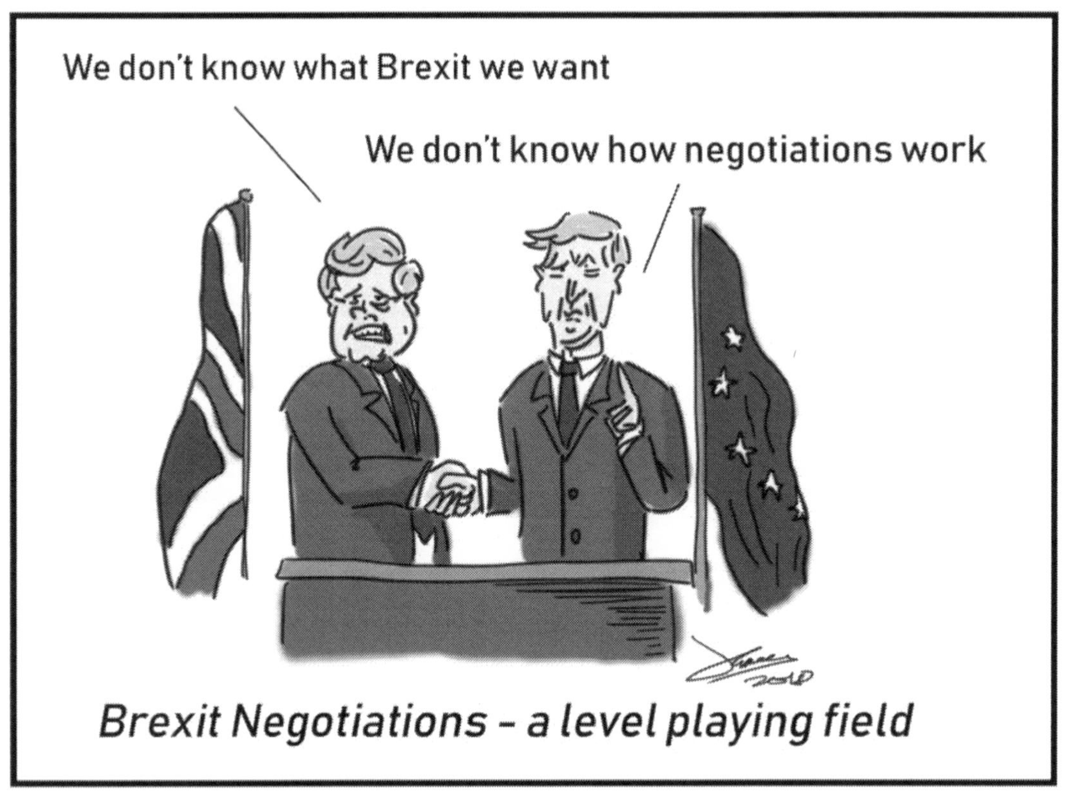
We don't know what Brexit we want
We don't know how negotiations work

Brexit Negotiations – a level playing field

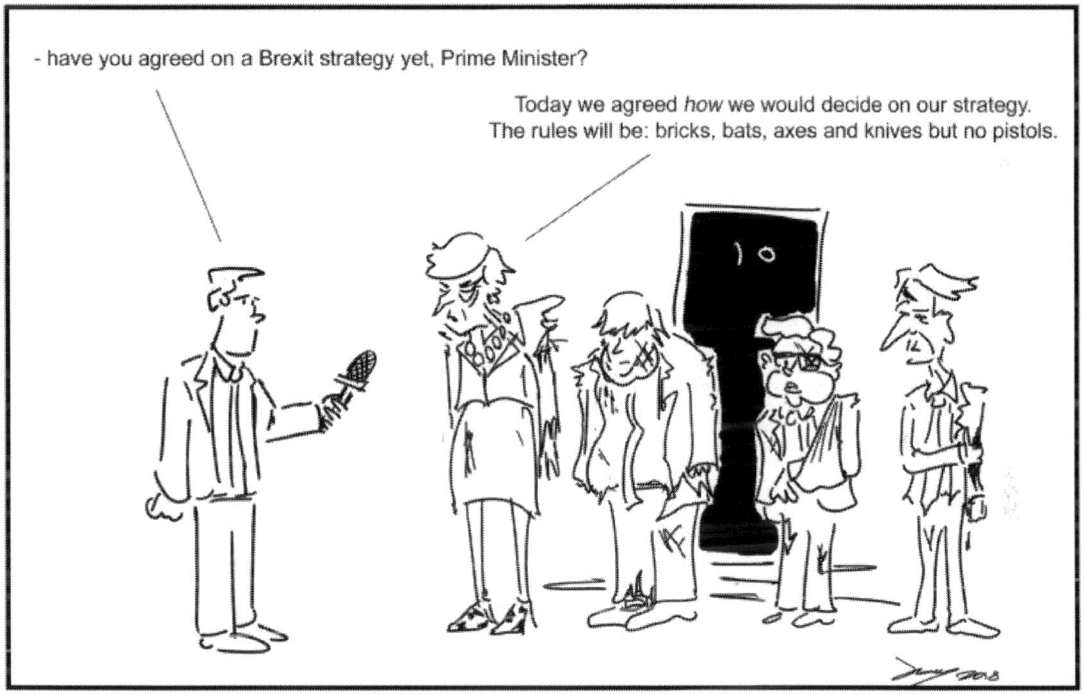
- have you agreed on a Brexit strategy yet, Prime Minister?
Today we agreed *how* we would decide on our strategy.
The rules will be: bricks, bats, axes and knives but no pistols.
10

The machine learning algorithm can't cope and the infinite number of monkeys are just churning out plays - so we're pulling letters from a scrabble bag
ERROR ERROR
Scientists race to create workable Brexit deal

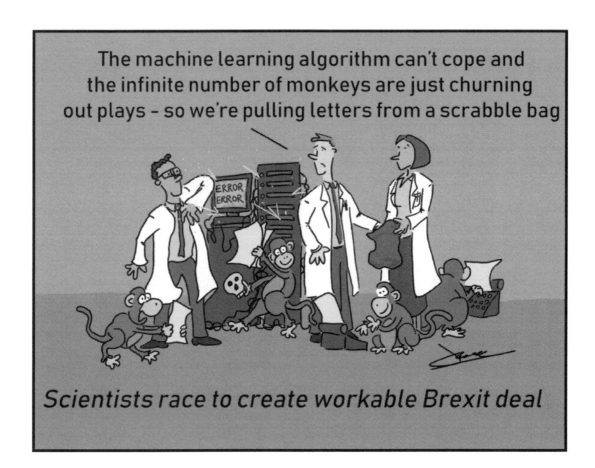

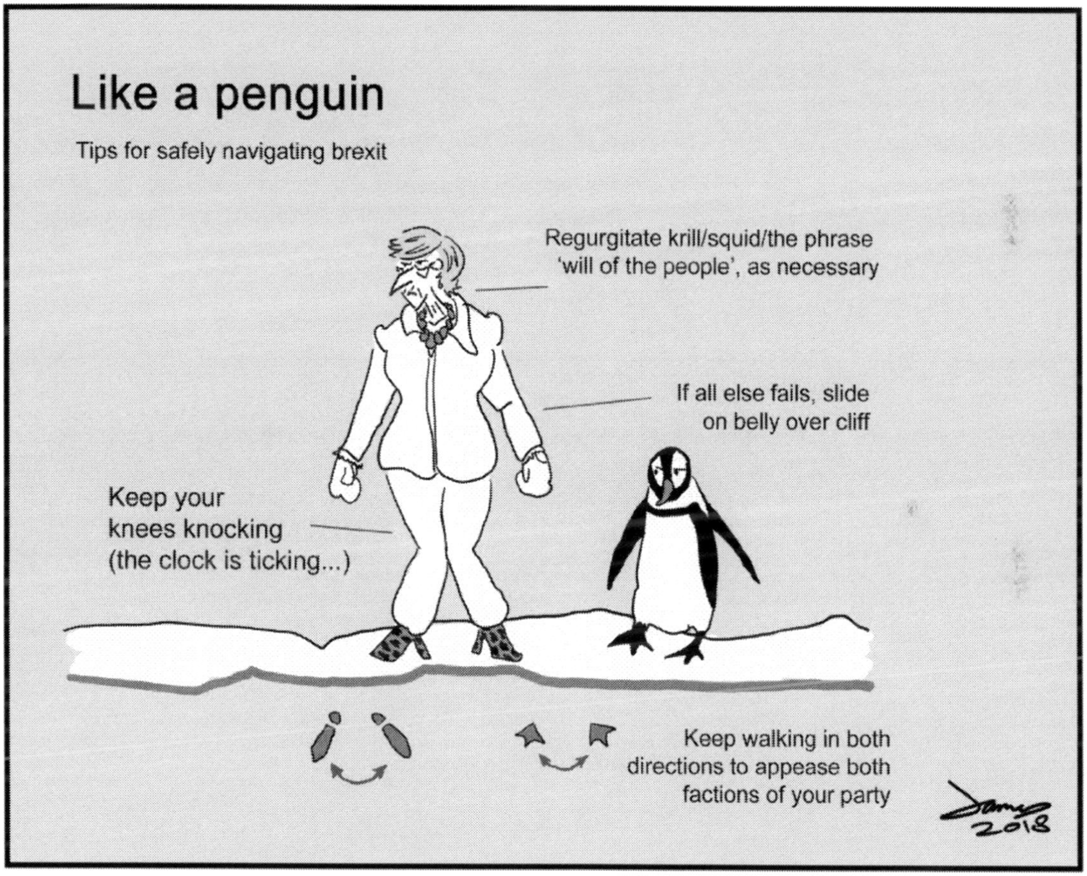
Like a penguin
Tips for safely navigating brexit
Regurgitate krill/squid/the phrase 'will of the people', as necessary
If all else fails, slide on belly over cliff
Keep your knees knocking (the clock is ticking...)
Keep walking in both directions to appease both factions of your party
2018

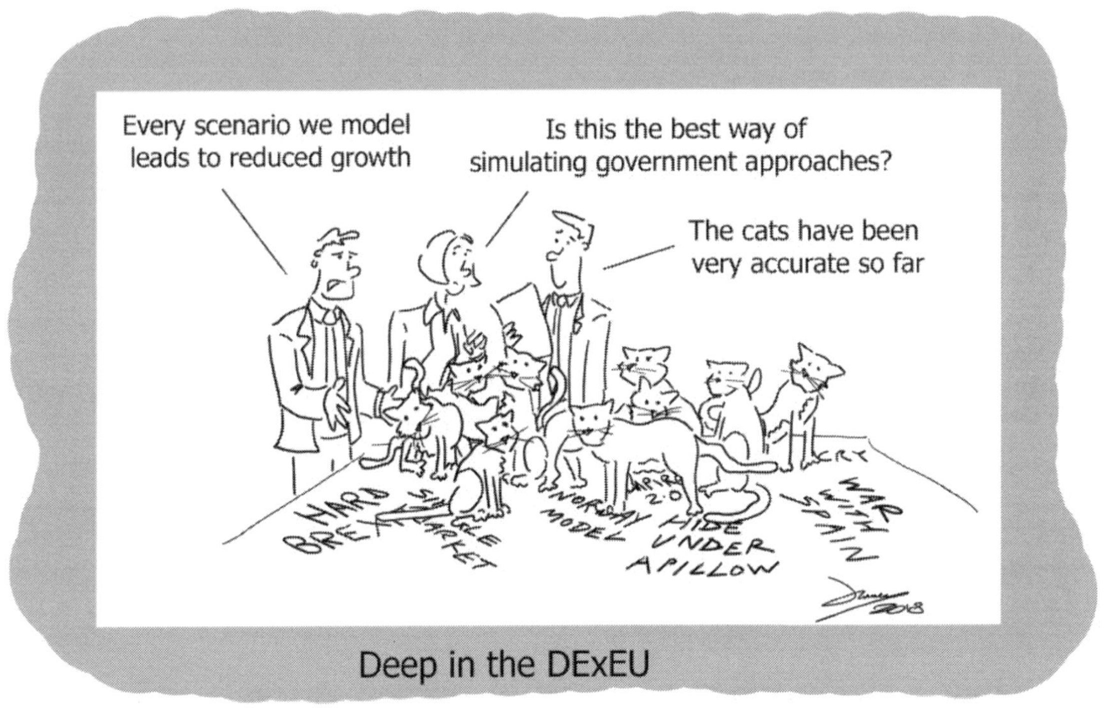

Every scenario we model leads to reduced growth
Is this the best way of simulating government approaches?
The cats have been very accurate so far
NORWAY MODEL
HIDE UNDER A PILLOW
WAR WITH SPAIN
CRY

Deep in the DExEU

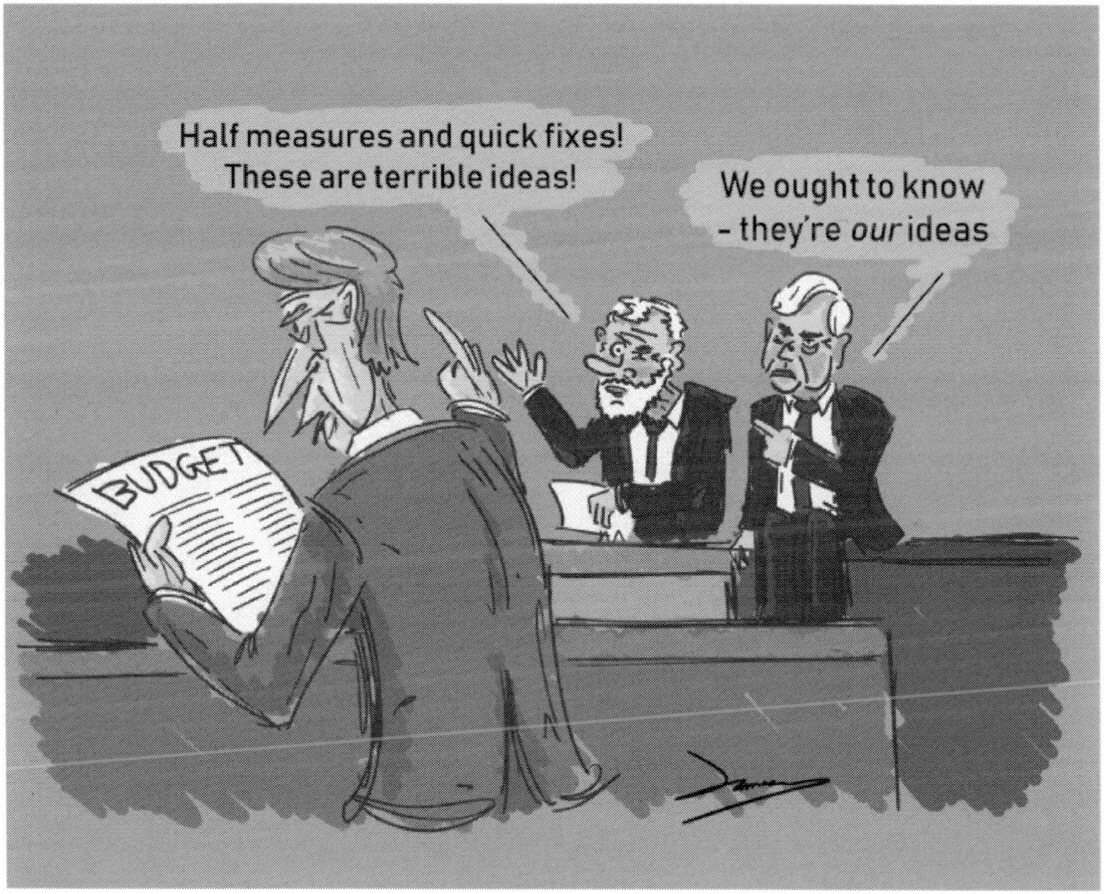
Half measures and quick fixes! These are terrible ideas!
We ought to know - they're *our* ideas
BUDGET

A Brexit Budget

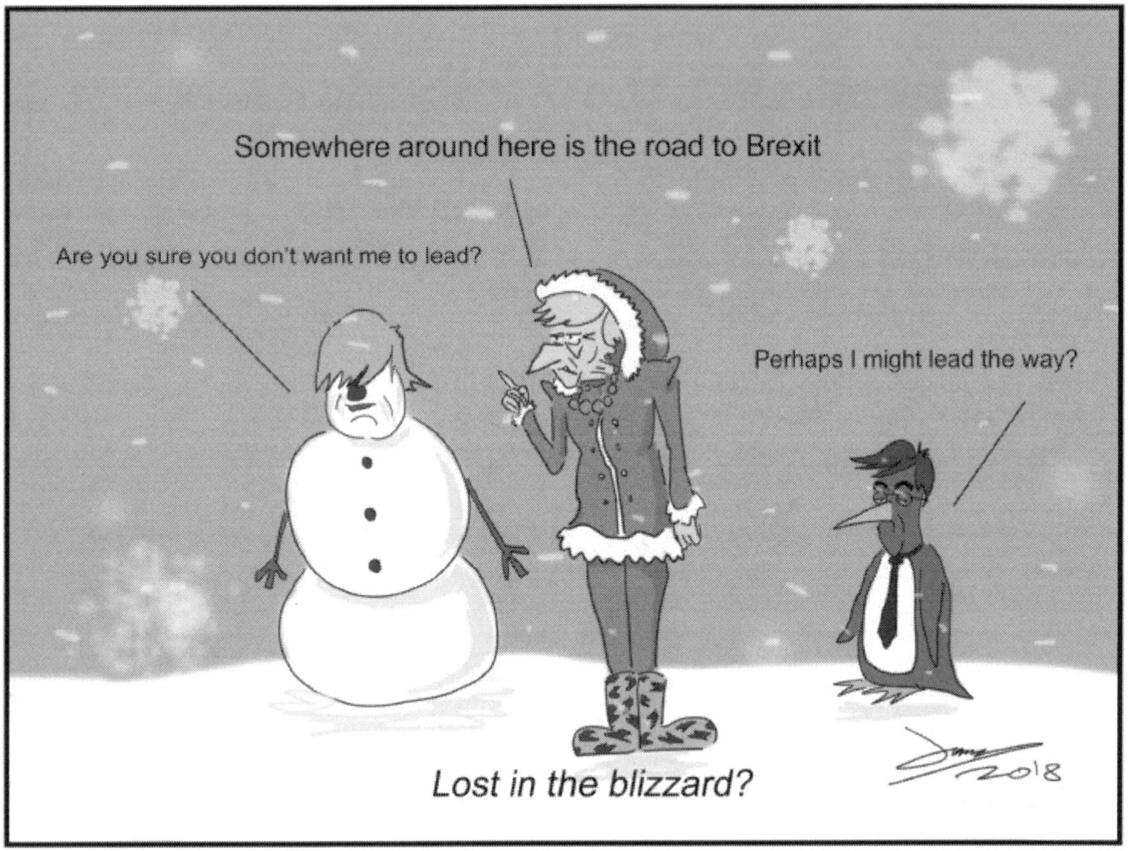
Are you sure you don't want me to lead?
Somewhere around here is the road to Brexit
Perhaps I might lead the way?
Lost in the blizzard?
2018

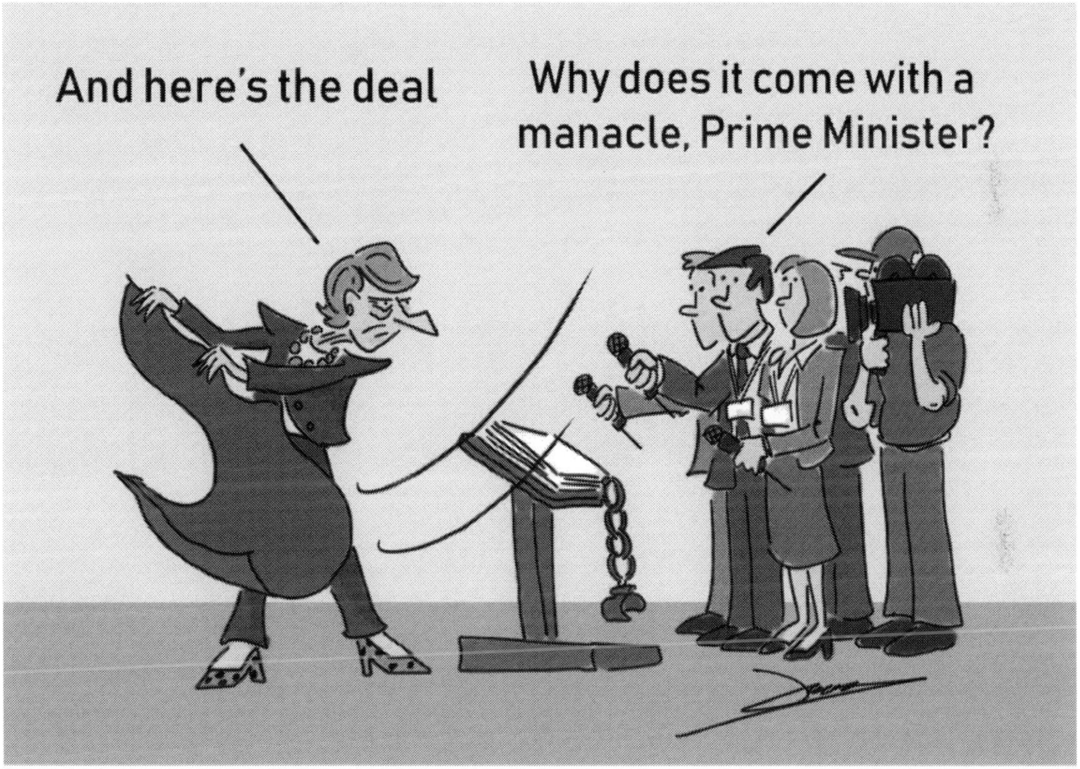
And here's the deal
Why does it come with a manacle, Prime Minister?

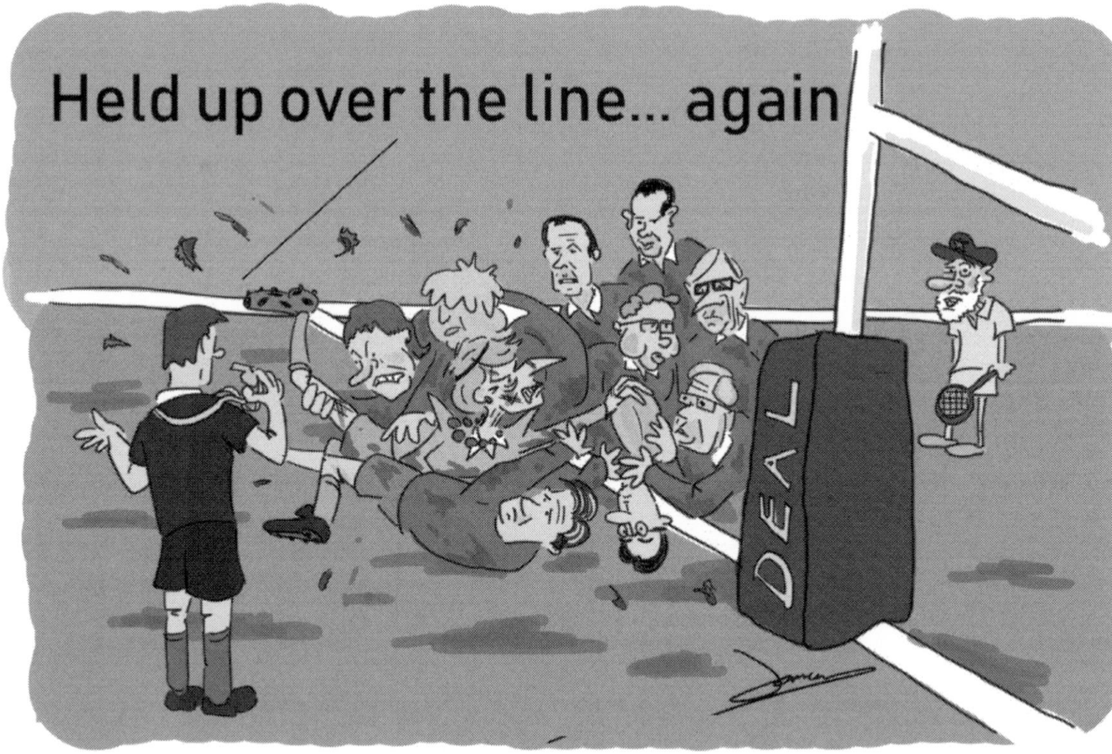
Held up over the line... again
DEAL

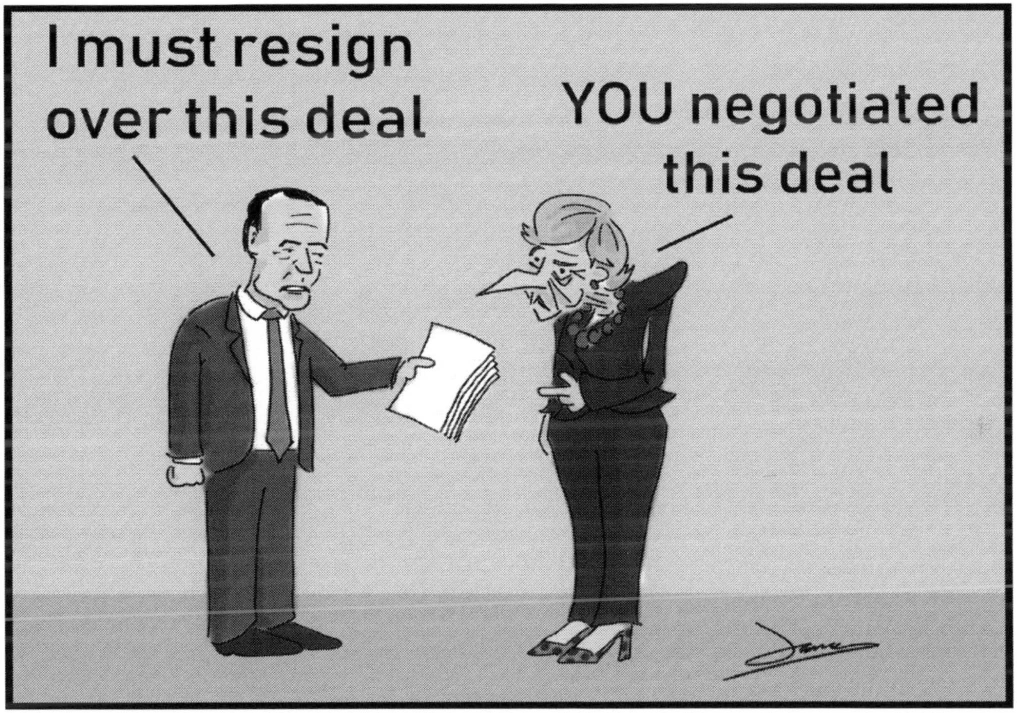
I must resign over this deal
YOU negotiated this deal

The Other Side

Unsurprisingly, many of the cartoons featured in this book focus on the Tory party. After all, Brexit is their baby. However, they are not the only ones deserving of a bit of ridicule. The Labour party's position on the biggest issue of the day is famously as clear as particularly opaque mud and the Liberal Democrats would like to stop Brexit with rude words.

The SNP see Brexit as a reason for Scotland to become independent. Though, for the SNP, remaining in the EU, eating an interesting breakfast or walking past a shrub would all be equally valid reasons for independence too.

Perhaps the most interesting developments in this area were the emergence of new parties. Labour begat T.I.G. who begat Change UK, which then paradoxically campaigned against change. The Brexit Party sprung up and split the leaver vote, thereby threatening to derail Brexit. New parties, same old bafflement.

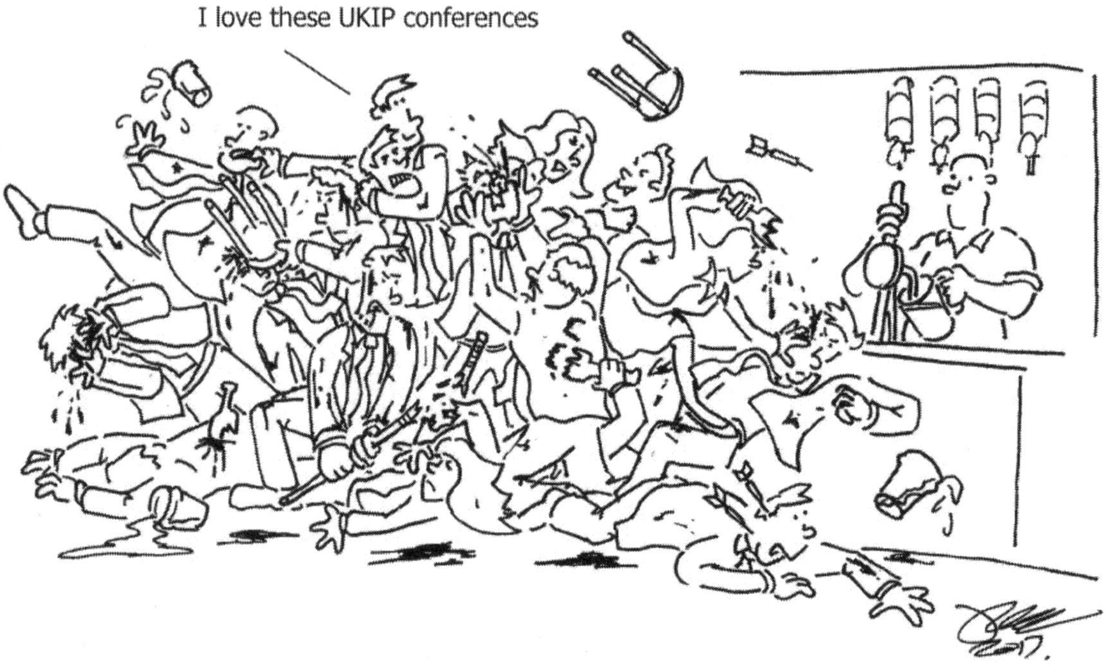
I love these UKIP conferences

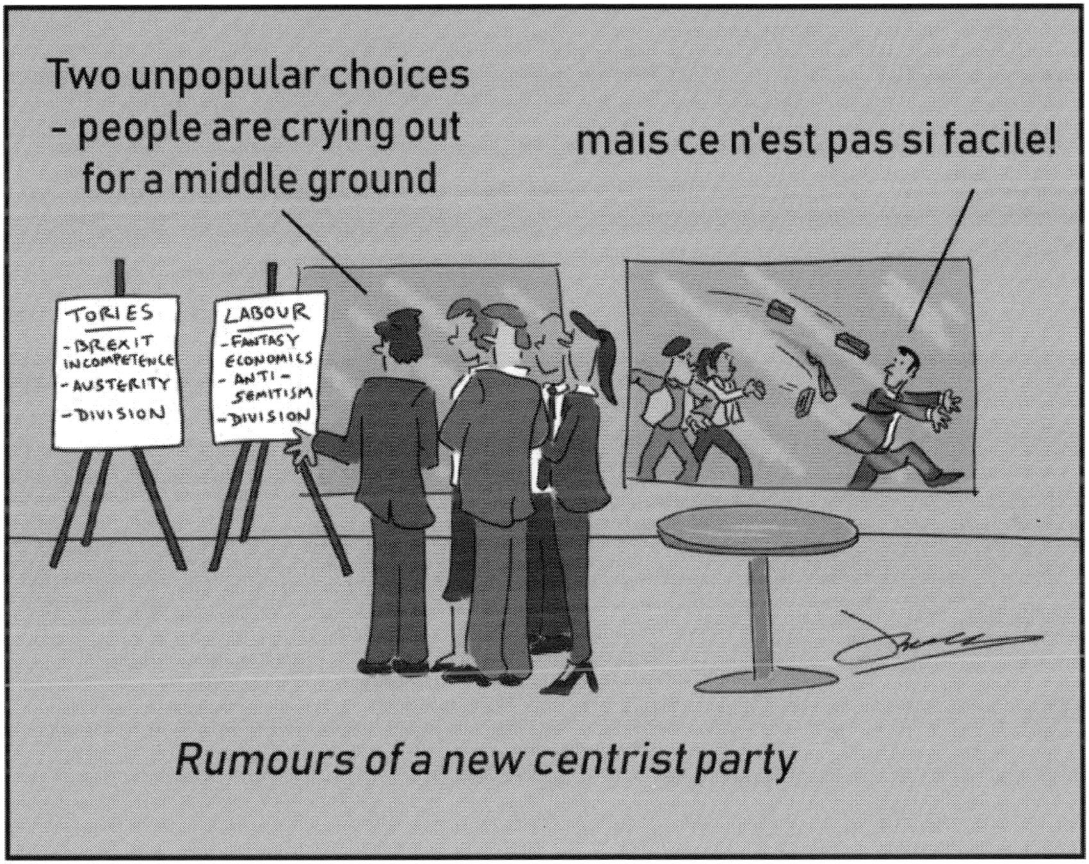
Two unpopular choices - people are crying out for a middle ground
mais ce n'est pas si facile!
TORIES
- BREXIT INCOMPETENCE
- AUSTERITY
- DIVISION
LABOUR
- FANTASY ECONOMICS
- ANTI-SEMITISM
- DIVISION

Rumours of a new centrist party

We're Corbyn Outriders!
Has anyone seen Jeremy?

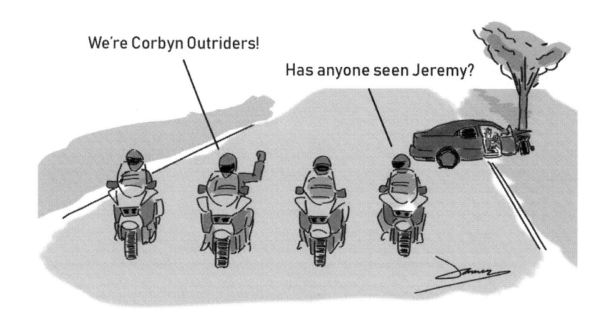

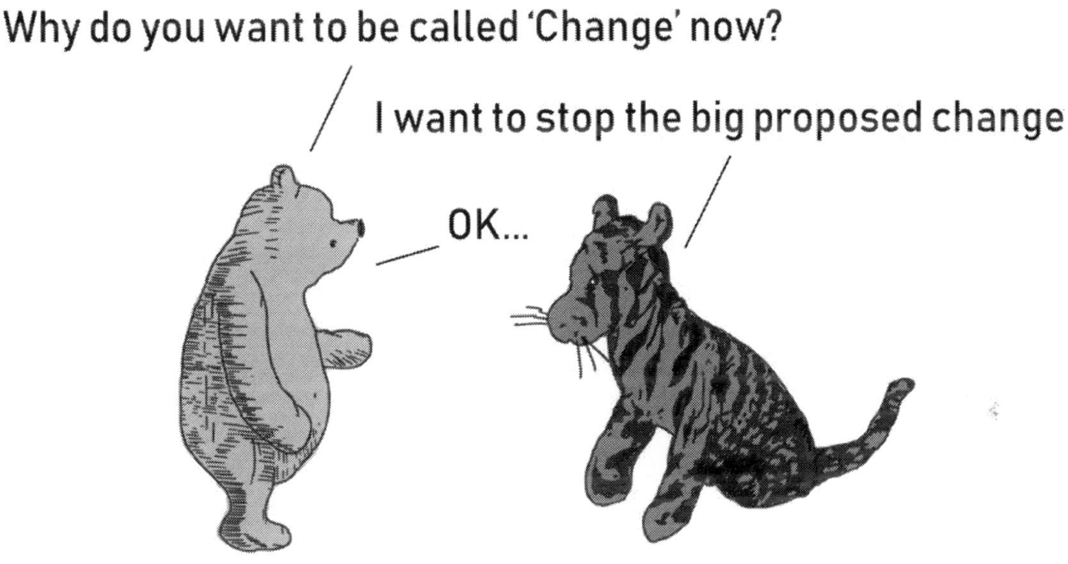
Why do you want to be called 'Change' now?
I want to stop the big proposed change
OK...

The wonderful thing about TIGgers

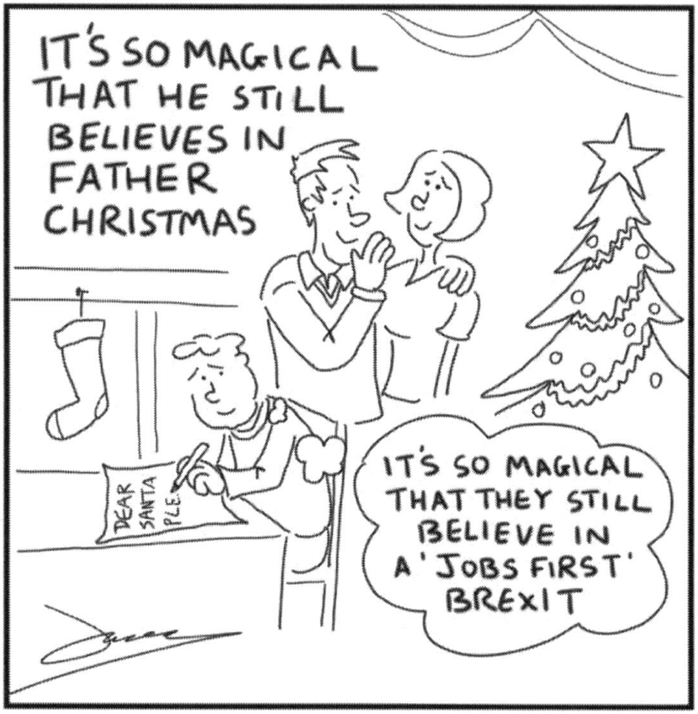
IT'S SO MAGICAL THAT HE STILL BELIEVES IN FATHER CHRISTMAS
DEAR SANTA PLE.
IT'S SO MAGICAL THAT THEY STILL BELIEVE IN A 'JOBS FIRST' BREXIT

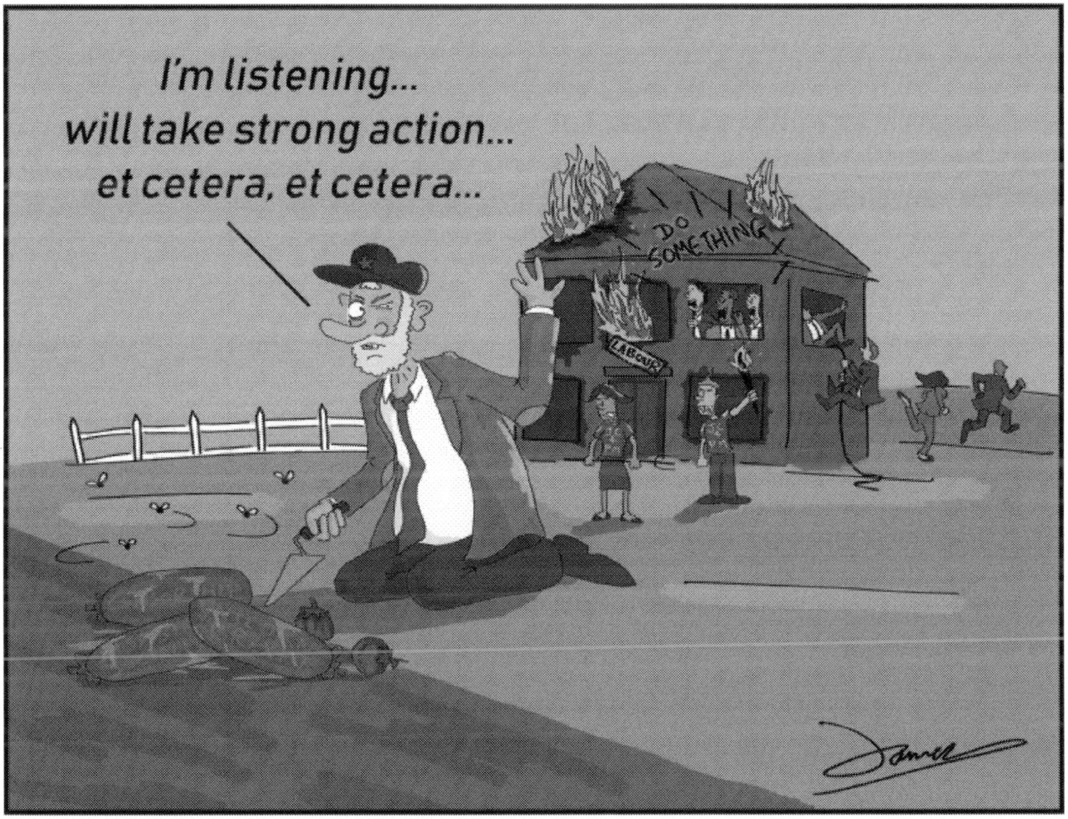
I'm listening...
will take strong action...
et cetera, et cetera...
DO SOMETHING

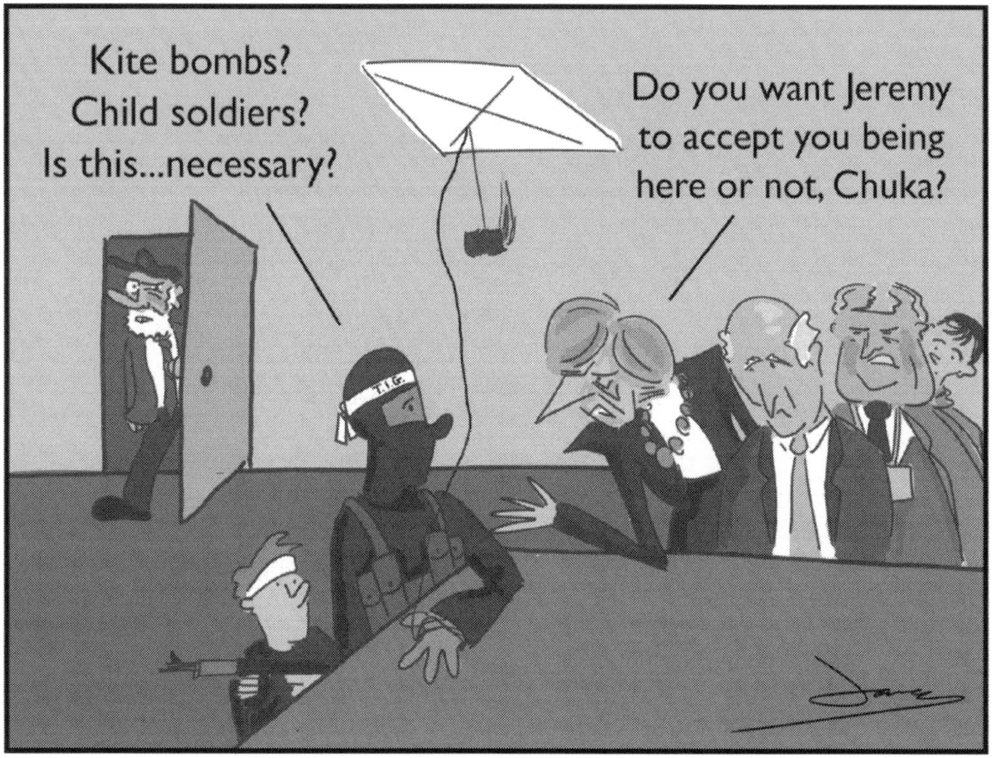
Kite bombs?
Child soldiers?
Is this...necessary?
Do you want Jeremy
to accept you being
here or not, Chuka?
T.I.G.

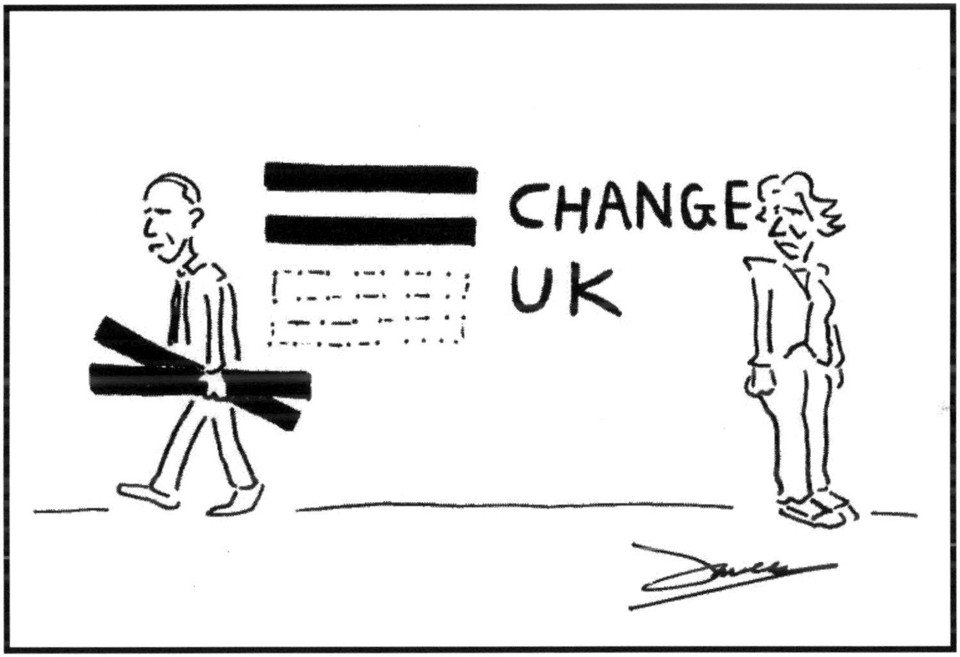
CHANGE
UK

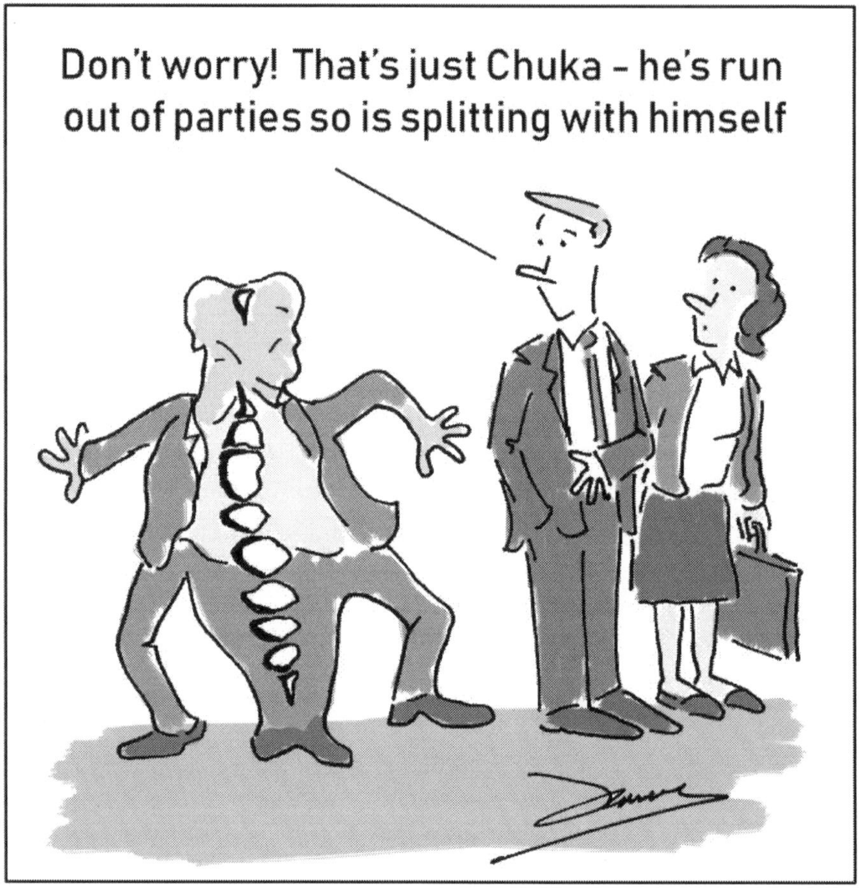
Don't worry! That's just Chuka – he's run out of parties so is splitting with himself

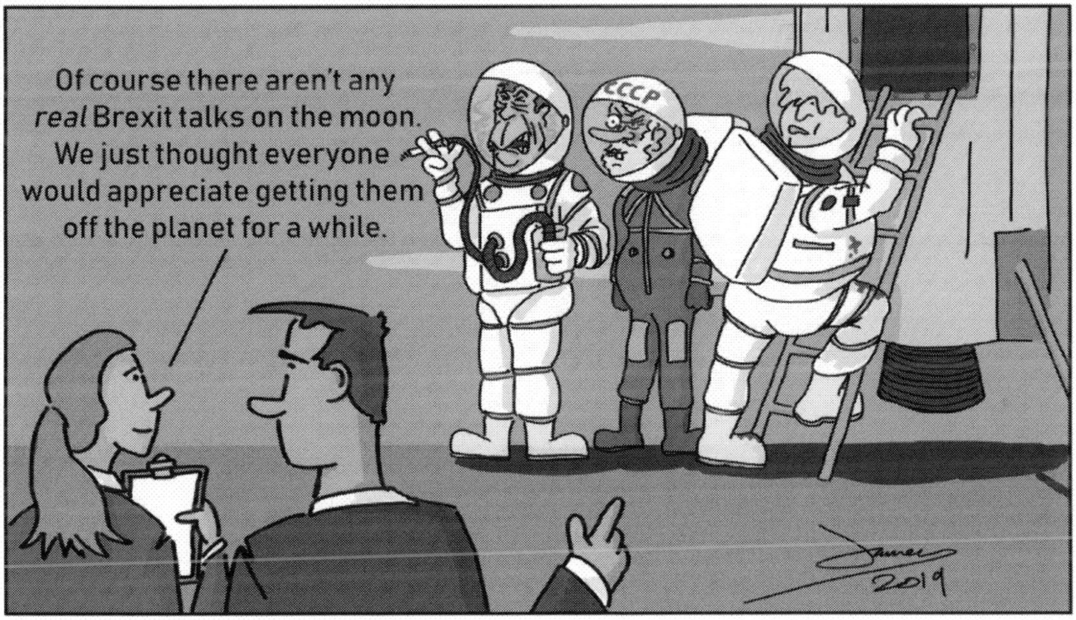
Of course there aren't any *real* Brexit talks on the moon. We just thought everyone would appreciate getting them off the planet for a while.
CCCP
2019

Project Fear?

What would the impact of Brexit be? Should you give up the thought of ever driving in Kent again, start stockpiling your favourite foods, or begin marinating your pets so they taste better when the time comes? At the time of writing, the potential impact of Brexit is hard to gauge.

There are without doubt many possible consequences that were either unforeseen or not given enough thought during the referendum campaign. However, the constant barrage of nightmare predictions about monsters rising from the deep and the sun being blotted out in the event of one country leaving a trading bloc made it difficult to ascertain the scare stories worth listening to.

The idea of a post-Brexit UK reminiscent of Mad Max but filled with biker gangs warring over the last few jars of marmite seems far-fetched. But perhaps it will turn out to be a rather tame prophecy.

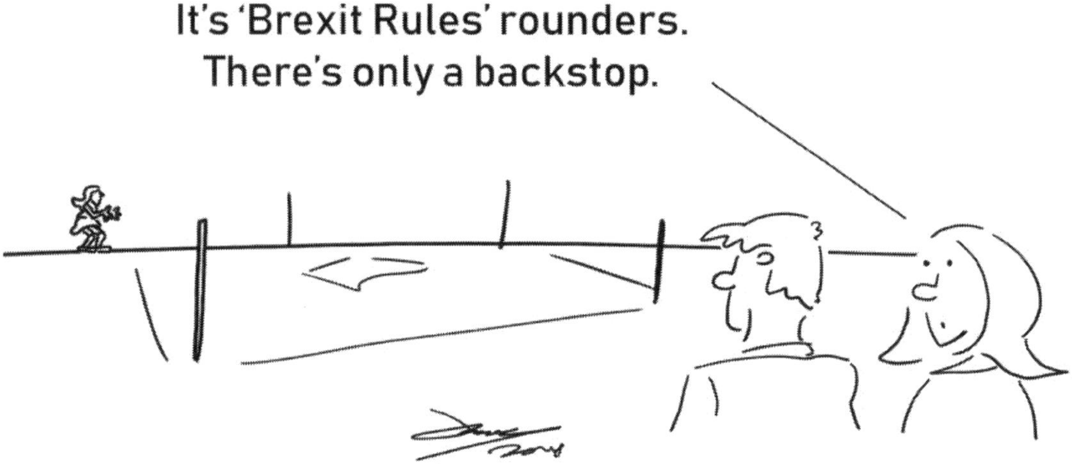
It's 'Brexit Rules' rounders.
There's only a backstop.

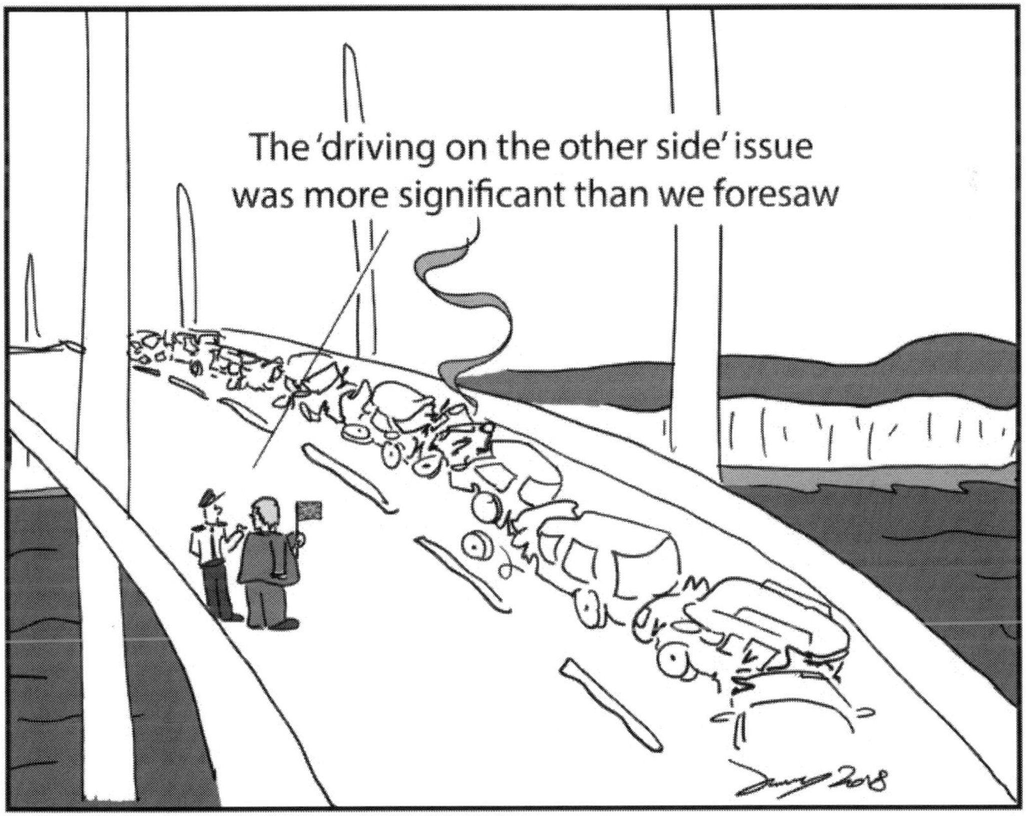
The 'driving on the other side' issue was more significant than we foresaw
Jenny 2018

England expects that every fisherman will do his duty

We live in British Waters again?
But I've always felt primarily European!

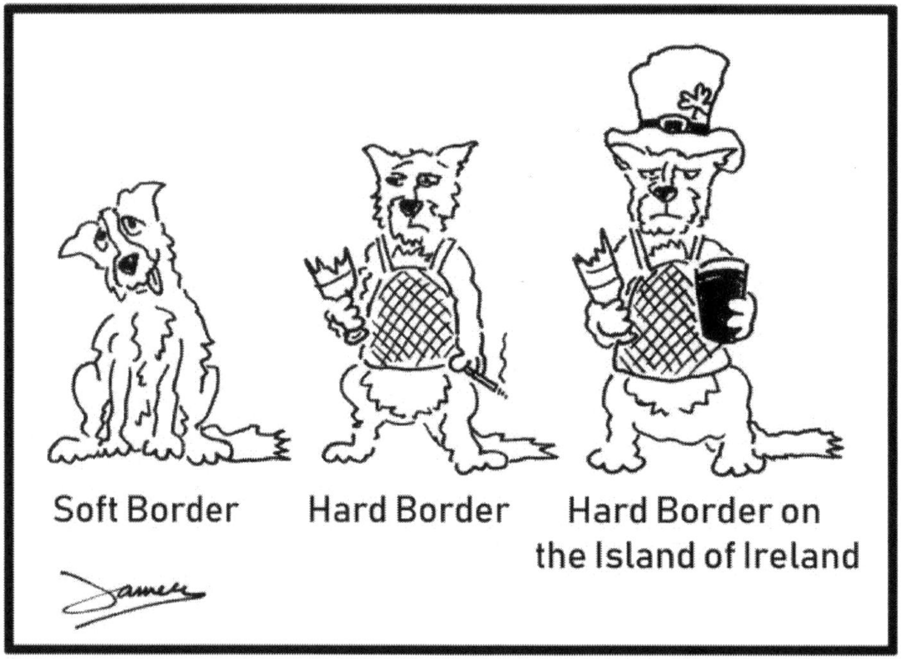
Soft Border
Hard Border
Hard Border on the Island of Ireland

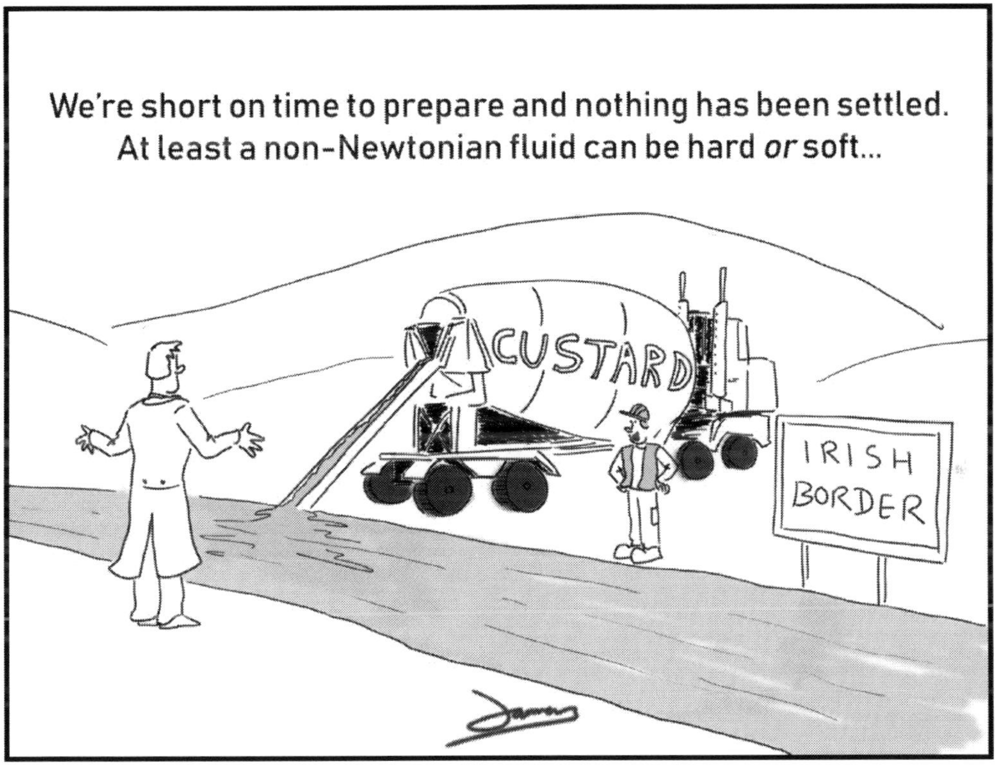
We're short on time to prepare and nothing has been settled.
At least a non-Newtonian fluid can be hard *or* soft...
CUSTARD
IRISH BORDER

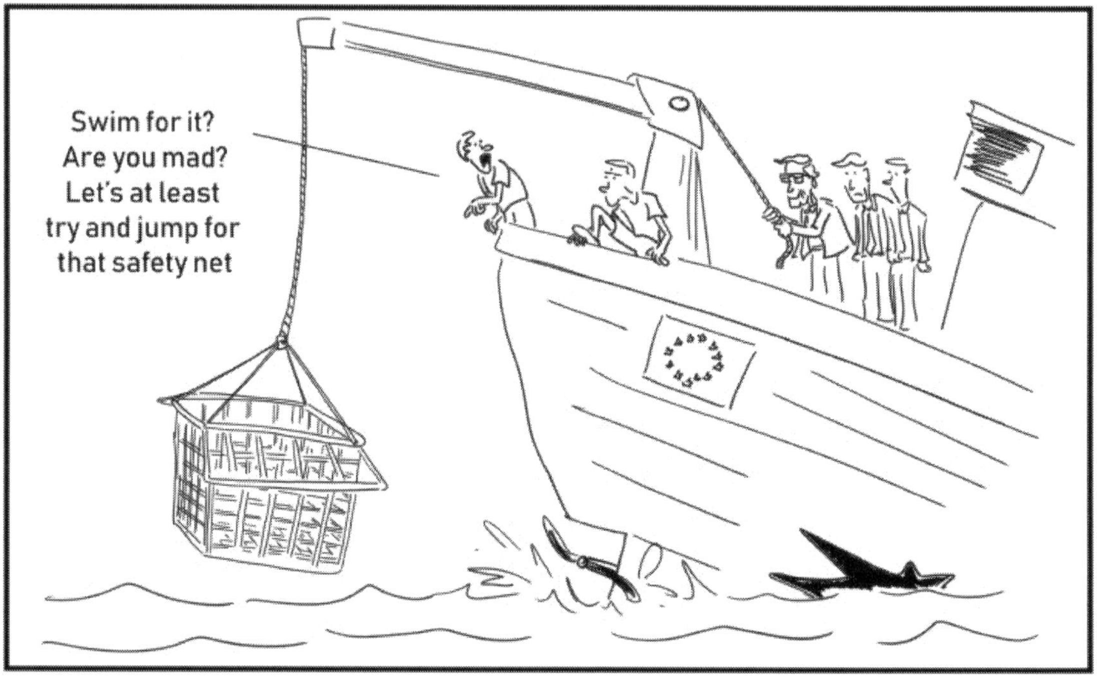
Swim for it? Are you mad? Let's at least try and jump for that safety net

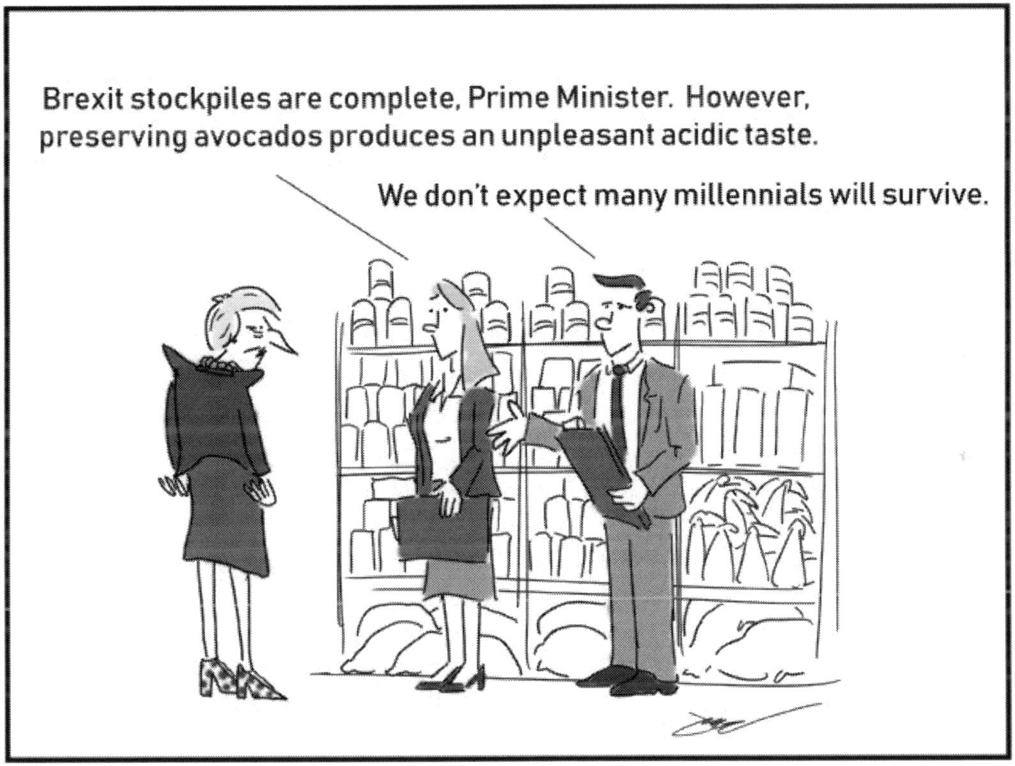
Brexit stockpiles are complete, Prime Minister. However, preserving avocados produces an unpleasant acidic taste.
We don't expect many millennials will survive.

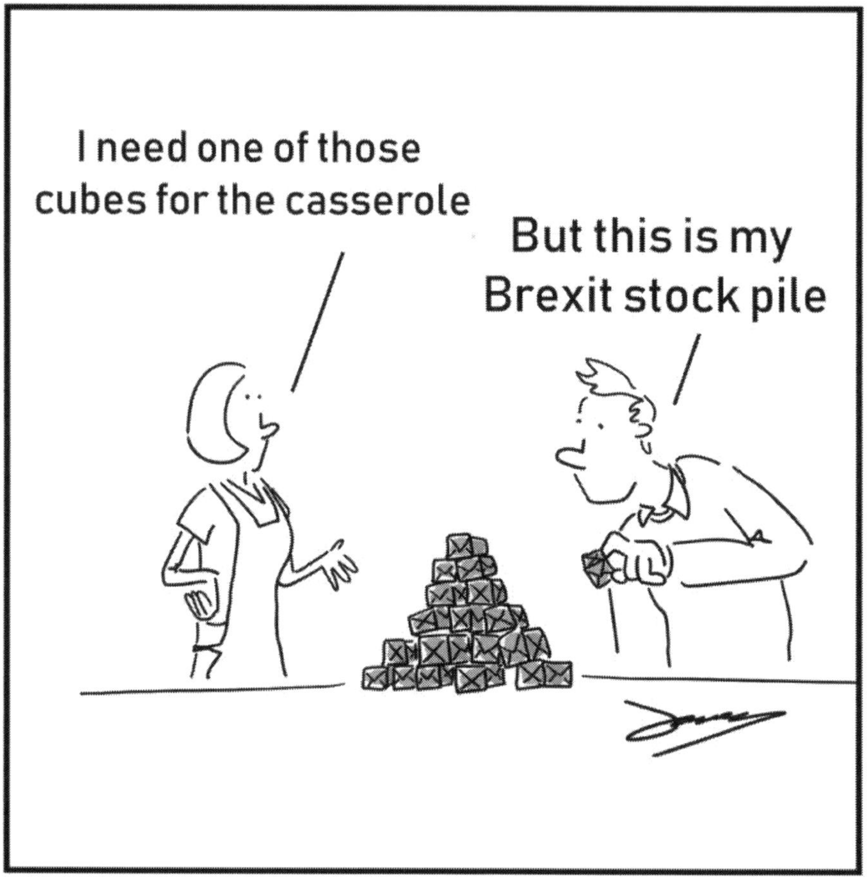
I need one of those cubes for the casserole
But this is my Brexit stock pile

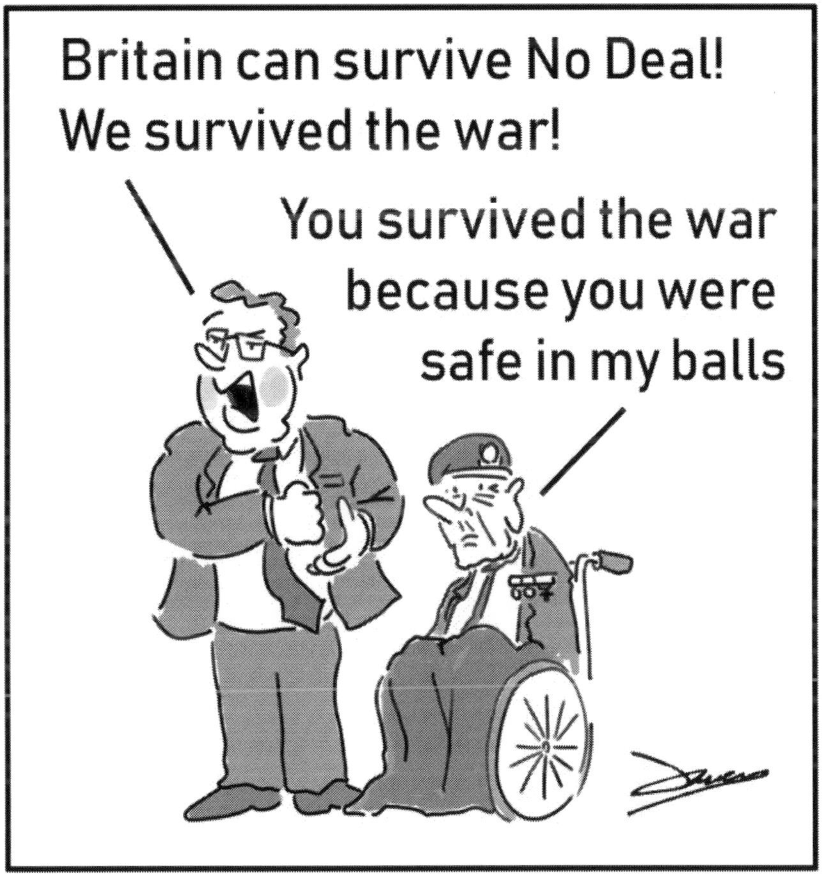
Britain can survive No Deal!
We survived the war!
You survived the war because you were safe in my balls

Winter of Discontent

Against all expectations, a Brexit deal was somehow cobbled together in 2018. It severed enough ties with the EU to allow the UK to fully participate on the global stage as an independent trading nation – freed from European shackles. It also maintained friendly accord with our continental neighbours, ensuring future security and integrity – especially on the island of Ireland. It brought both sides together, healed divisions and has largely been regarded ever since as a political masterstroke.

Not really. It was a fudgy compromise, so naturally MPs on either side hated it and it bombed.

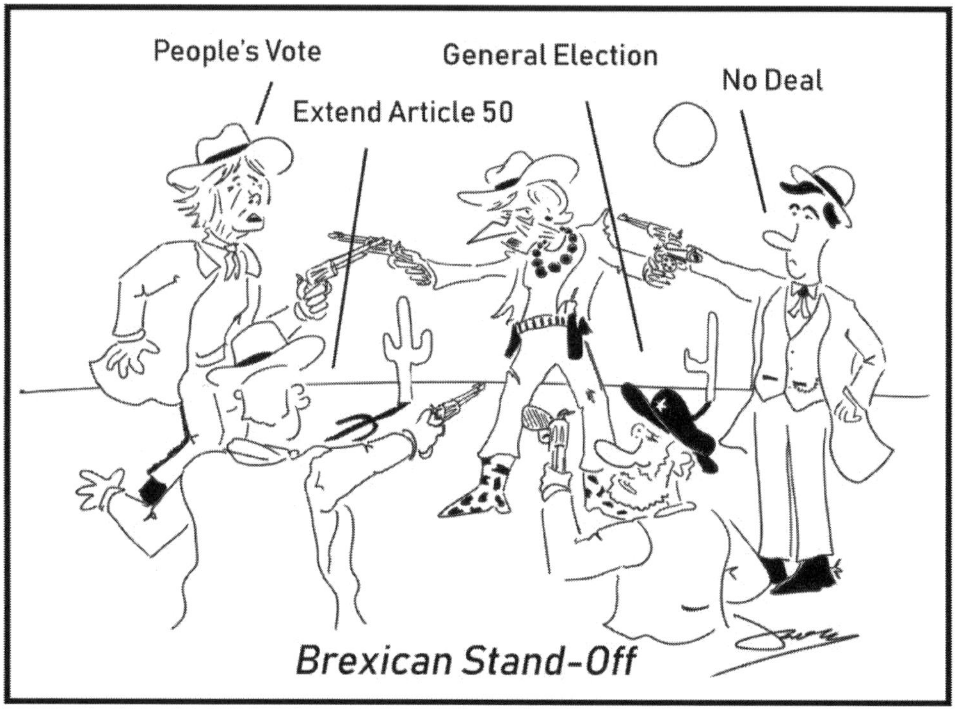
People's Vote
Extend Article 50
General Election
No Deal

Brexican Stand-Off

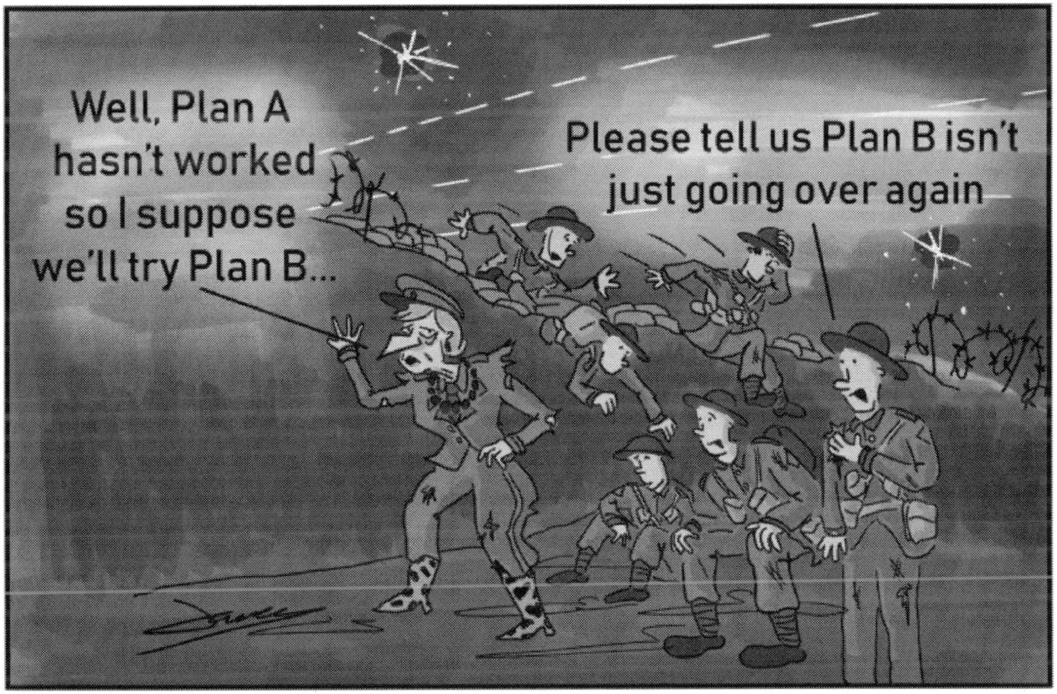
Well, Plan A hasn't worked so I suppose we'll try Plan B...
Please tell us Plan B isn't just going over again

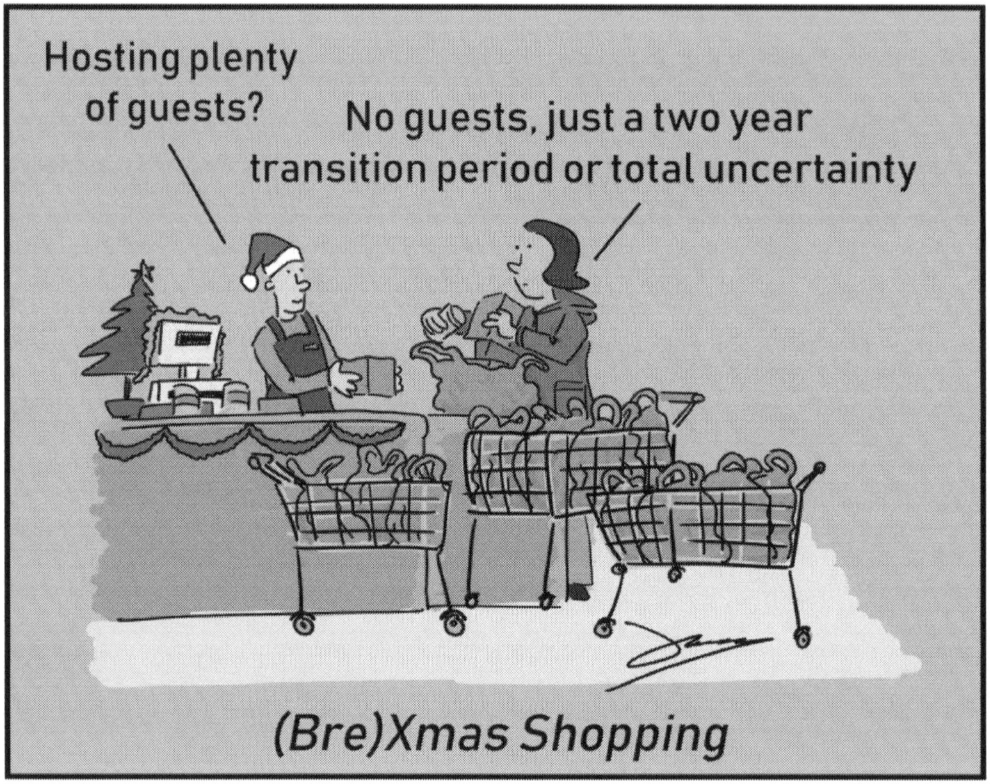
Hosting plenty of guests?
No guests, just a two year transition period or total uncertainty

(Bre)Xmas Shopping

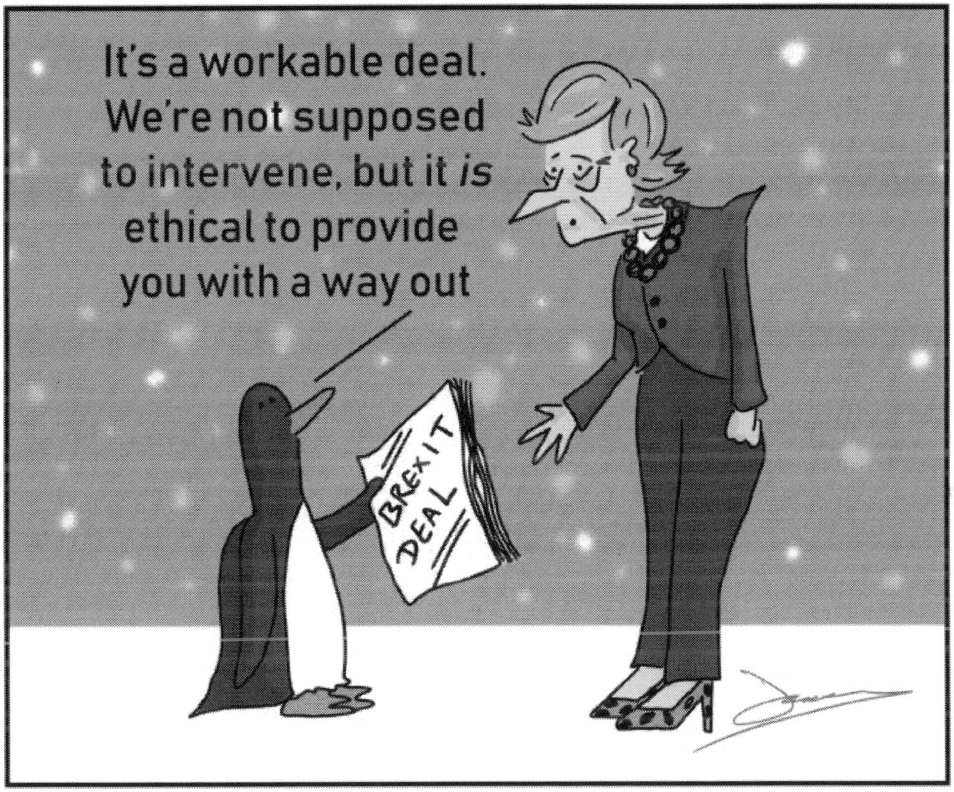
It's a workable deal. We're not supposed to intervene, but it *is* ethical to provide you with a way out
BREXIT DEAL

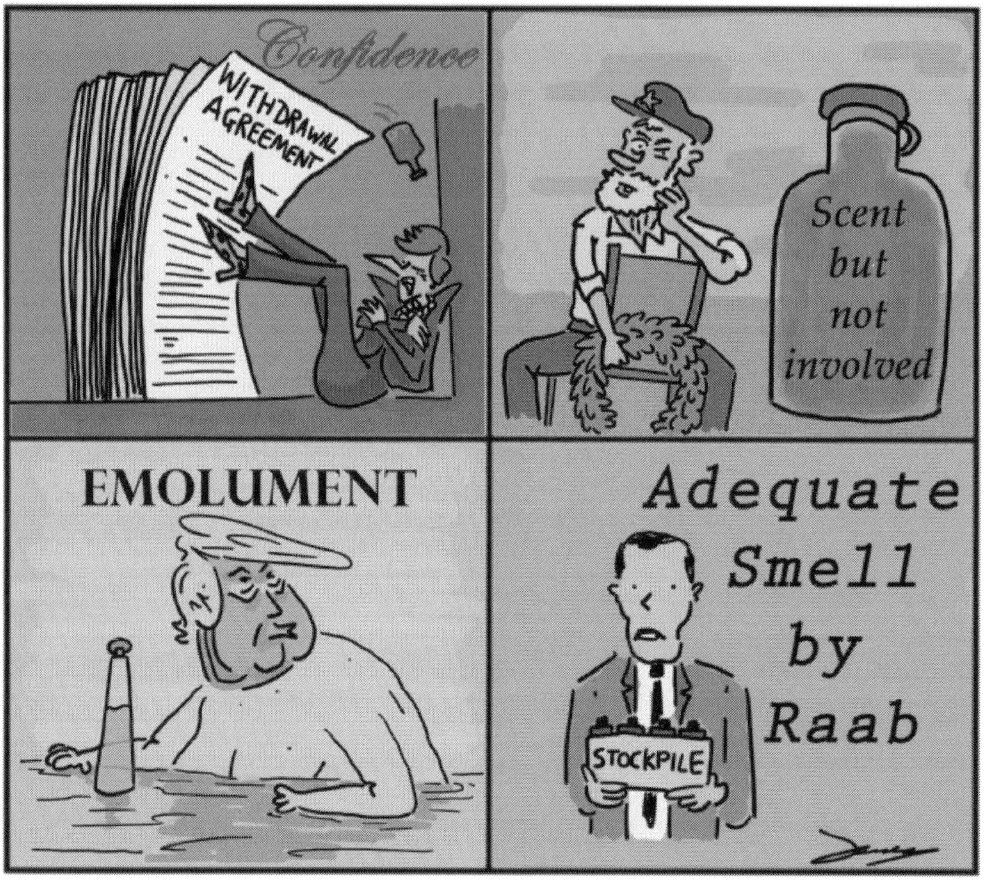
Confidence
WITHDRAWAL AGREEMENT
Scent but not involved
EMOLUMENT
Adequate Smell by Raab
STOCKPILE

New Fragrances

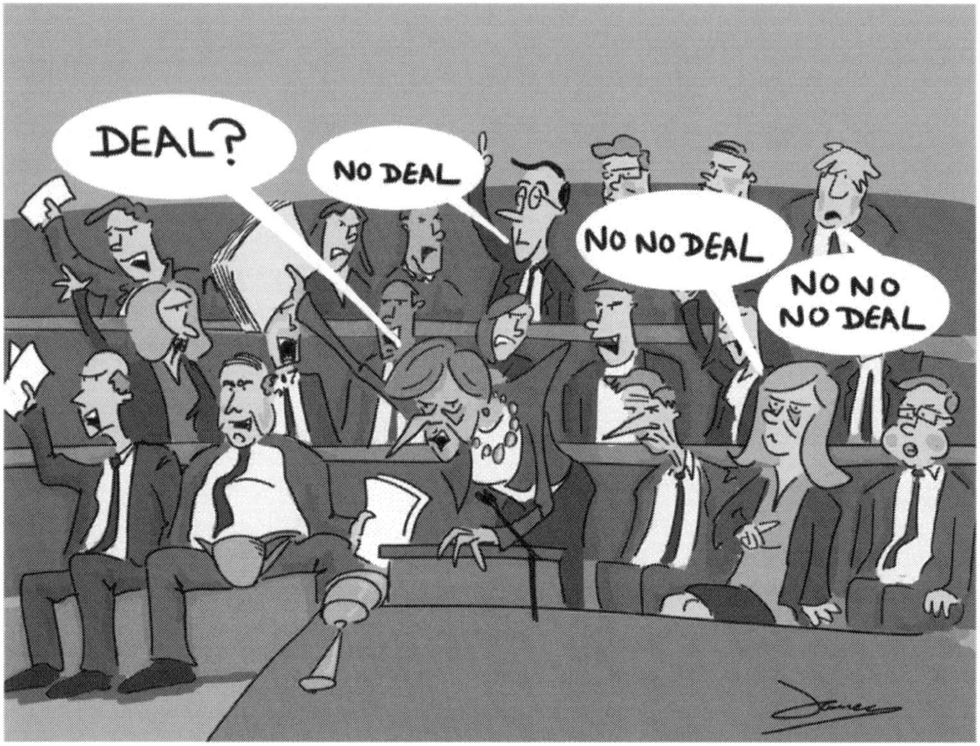
DEAL?
NO DEAL
NO NO DEAL
NO NO
NO DEAL

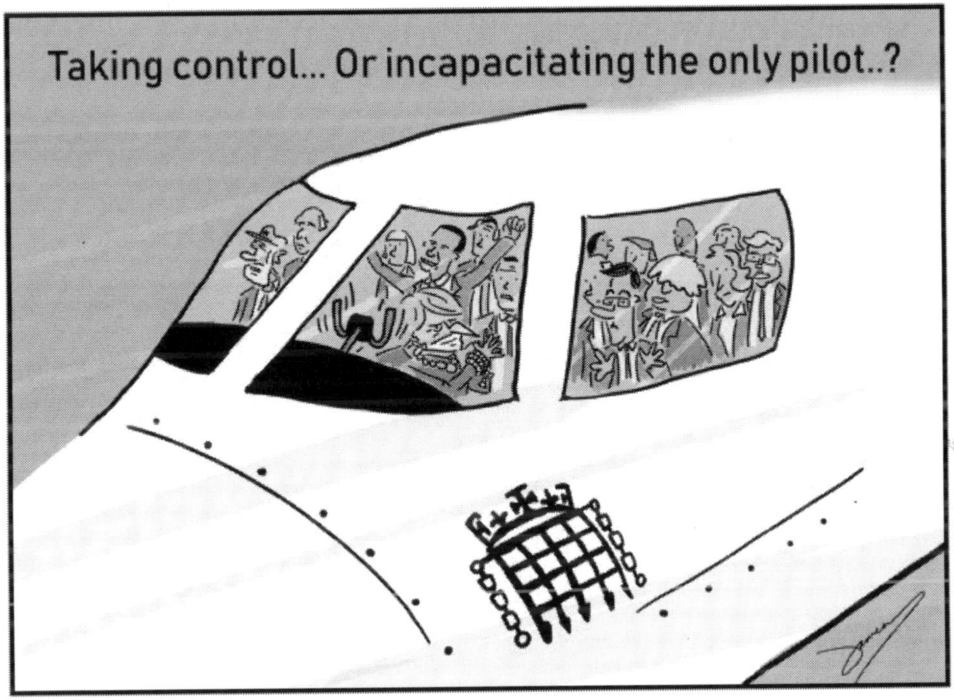
Taking control... Or incapacitating the only pilot..?

Countdown to Brexit Day

"Take 'No Deal' off the table" was the refrain in the months, weeks, and days leading up to our grand departure date. Sensible advice. Who would want to crash out of the EU with no deal in place to cover all the many intertwined links we have? Also very stupid advice when you remember that 'No Deal' is the table.

There's a fine line between high drama and high farce, and this period of time crossed well over that line towards the latter. A particular lowlight was the bold move by MPs to SEIZE CONTROL of the agenda, conduct a series of indicative votes, and discover that they didn't want to carry out any of the options they had proposed.

All manner of colluding and chicanery was taking place to pass a deal or to thwart that deal. And all that while the clock ticked down towards B-Day.

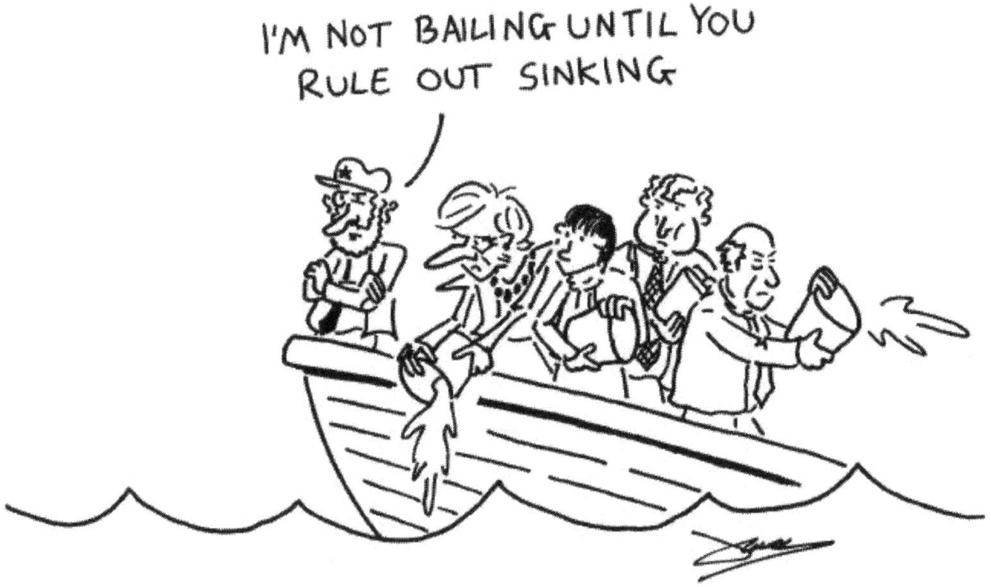
I'M NOT BAILING UNTIL YOU RULE OUT SINKING

I've made you dinner
No!
If you don't want this... is there a dinner you do want?
No!
So, no dinner?
I rule out no dinner
At least you'll make a great MP one day

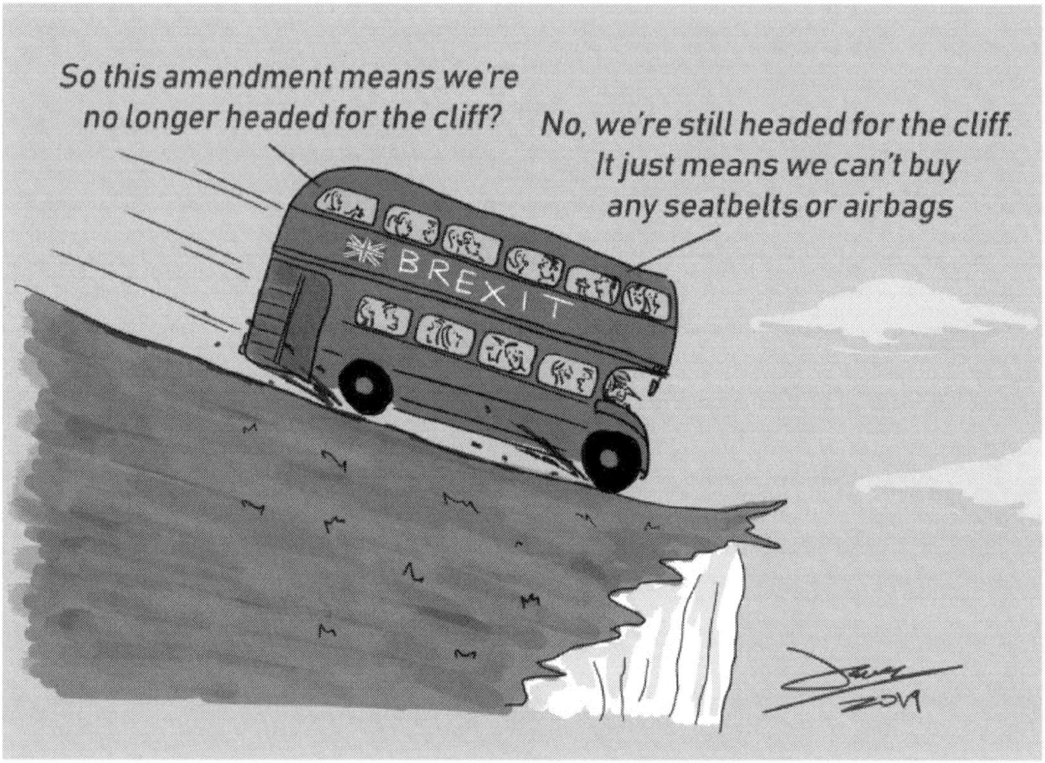
So this amendment means we're no longer headed for the cliff?
No, we're still headed for the cliff. It just means we can't buy any seatbelts or airbags
BREXIT

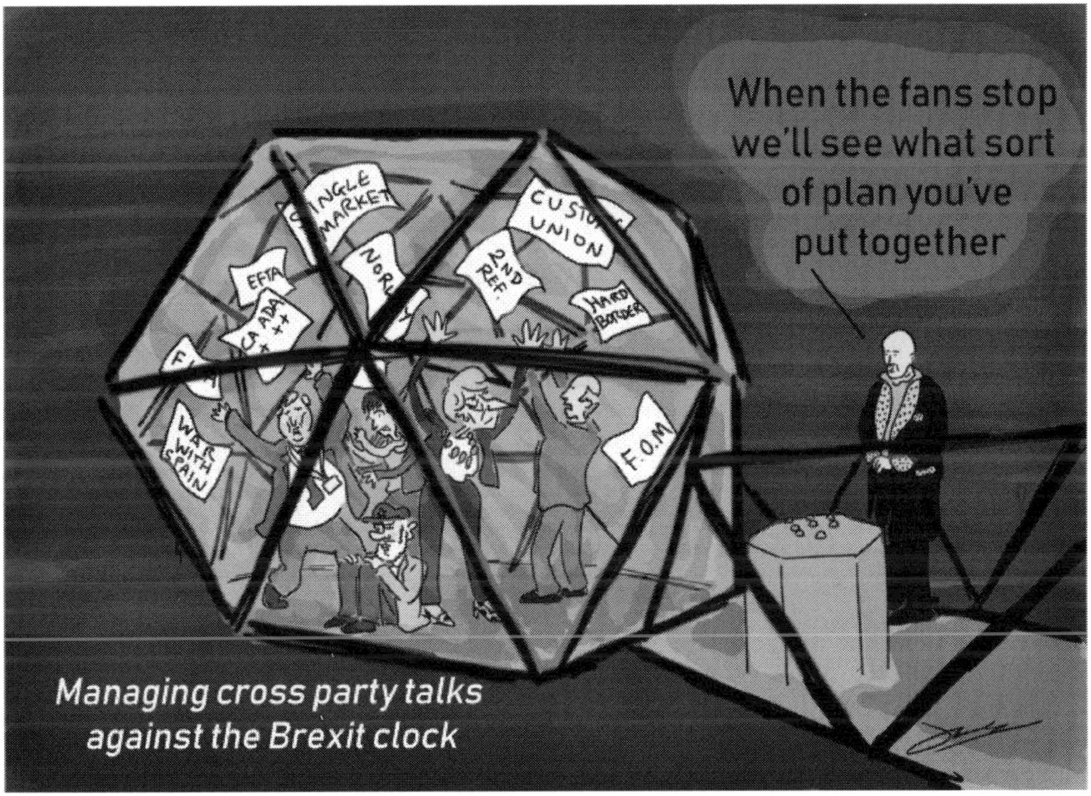
When the fans stop we'll see what sort of plan you've put together
EFTA
2ND REF.
HARD BORDER
UNION
WAR WITH SPAIN
F.O.M

Managing cross party talks against the Brexit clock

Good news, lads
- I've secured an extension for us

...and each Brexit option shall have a nominated champion...
It's not a perfect system,
but it might break the impasse
jamesmellorcreative.com

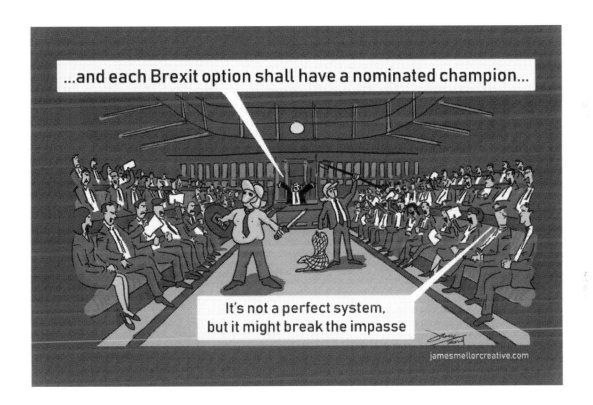

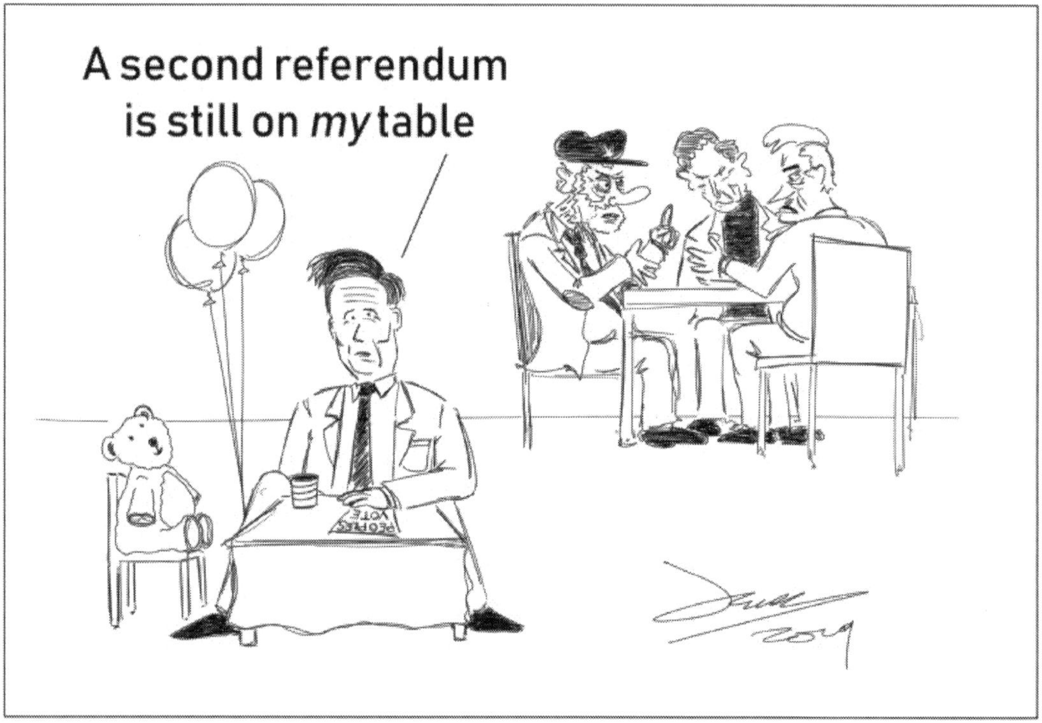
A second referendum
is still on *my* table
PEOPLES VOTE

Shadow Brexit Secretary

Don't drive *there!*
Don't go *there* either!
Don't *stay here!*
All you lot ever say is what you *don't* want
Boo! Let us drive! Let us drive! Let us drive! Let us drive!
o.k.
You're the driver. You own this mess.

jamesmellorcreative.com

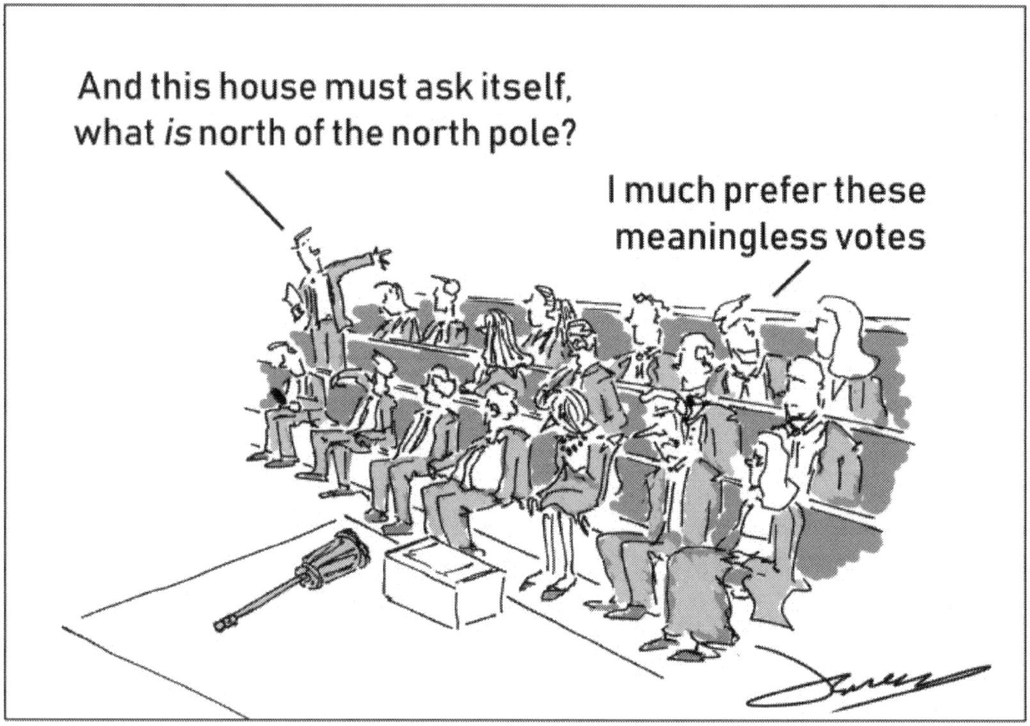
And this house must ask itself, what *is* north of the north pole?
I much prefer these meaningless votes

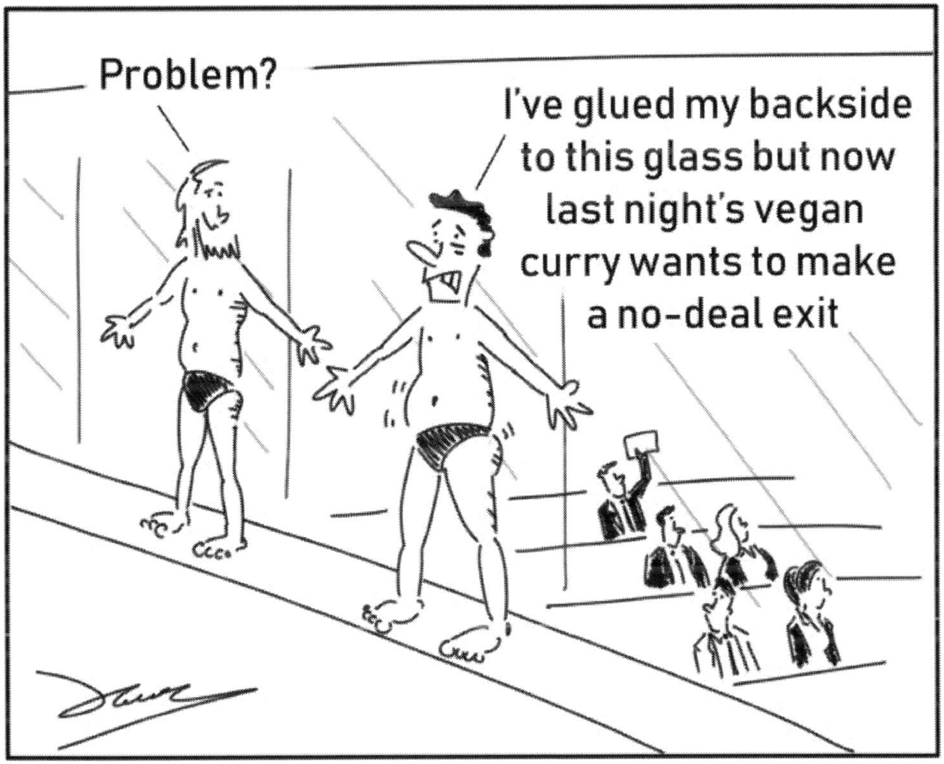

Problem?
I've glued my backside to this glass but now last night's vegan curry wants to make a no-deal exit

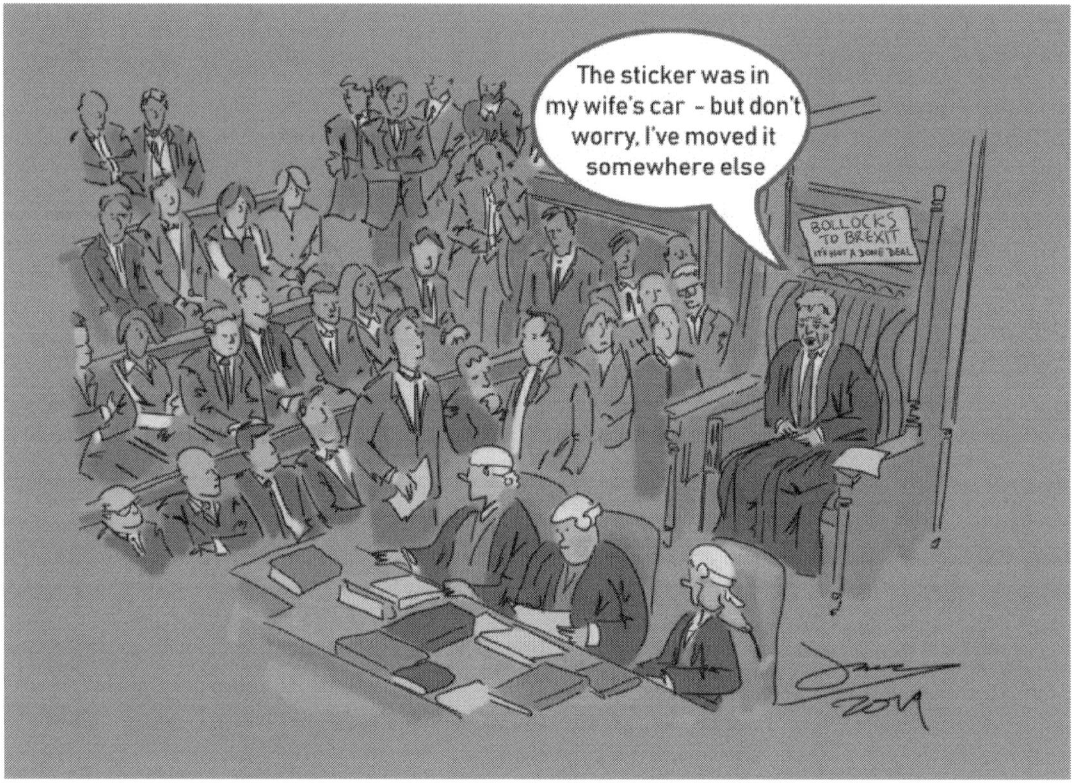
The sticker was in my wife's car - but don't worry, I've moved it somewhere else
BOLLOCKS TO BREXIT

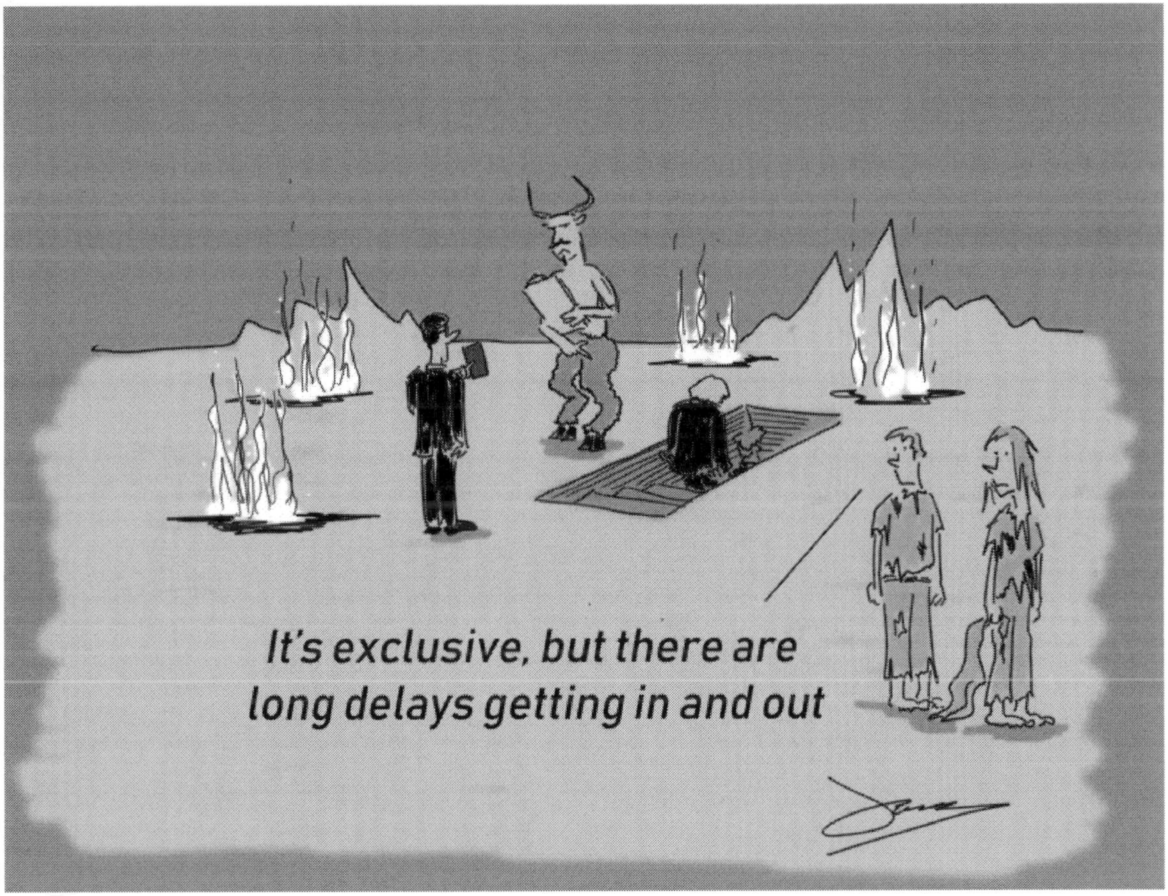
It's exclusive, but there are long delays getting in and out

Donald Tusk's 'special place in Hell' for Brexiteers

The Unfortunate Mrs May

Still here? But Brexit Day's been and gone! Oh. Ah, I see.

You can only kick the can so far before you have to carry it. The thumping rejection of Theresa May's negotiated Withdrawal Agreement had to catch up with her at some point. The fact it was the only deal on offer is a fact that perhaps still hasn't sunk in for some of the MPs involved in trashing it.

I'm going to miss drawing Prime Minister May. Her earnest and tragic efforts made her stand out from the cast of clowns. Like the only Ernie Wise in a building full of Eric Morecambes. Still ridiculous, but (almost) endearingly sincere.

Embedding 'No Deal is better than a bad deal' into the public mindset may have been a massive clanging error though.

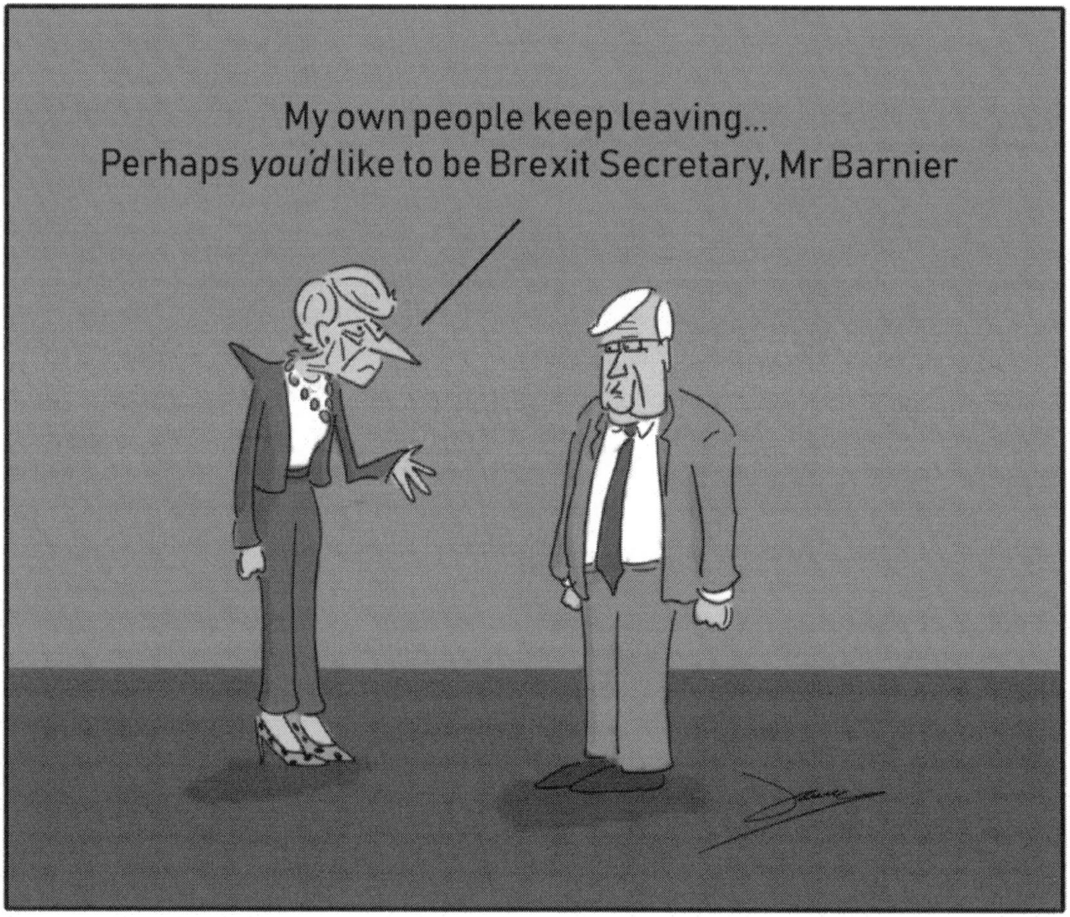
My own people keep leaving...
Perhaps *you'd* like to be Brexit Secretary, Mr Barnier

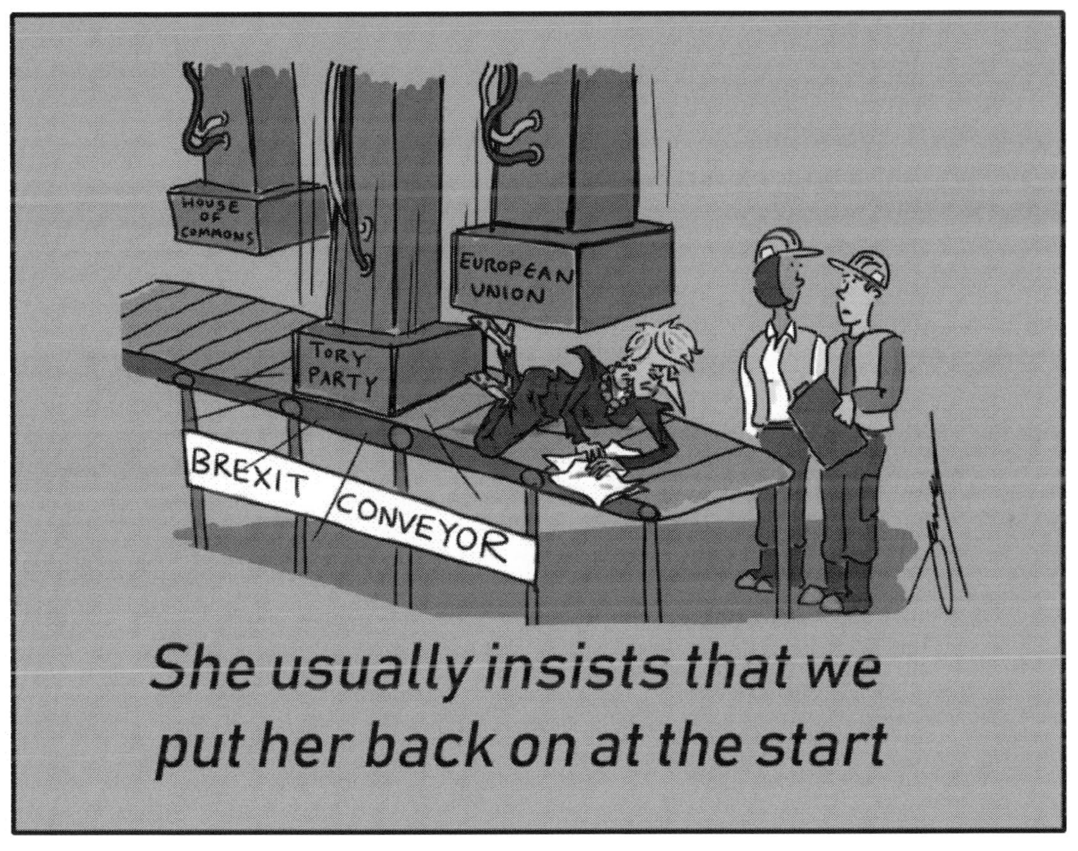
HOUSE OF COMMONS
TORY PARTY
EUROPEAN UNION
BREXIT CONVEYOR

She usually insists that we put her back on at the start

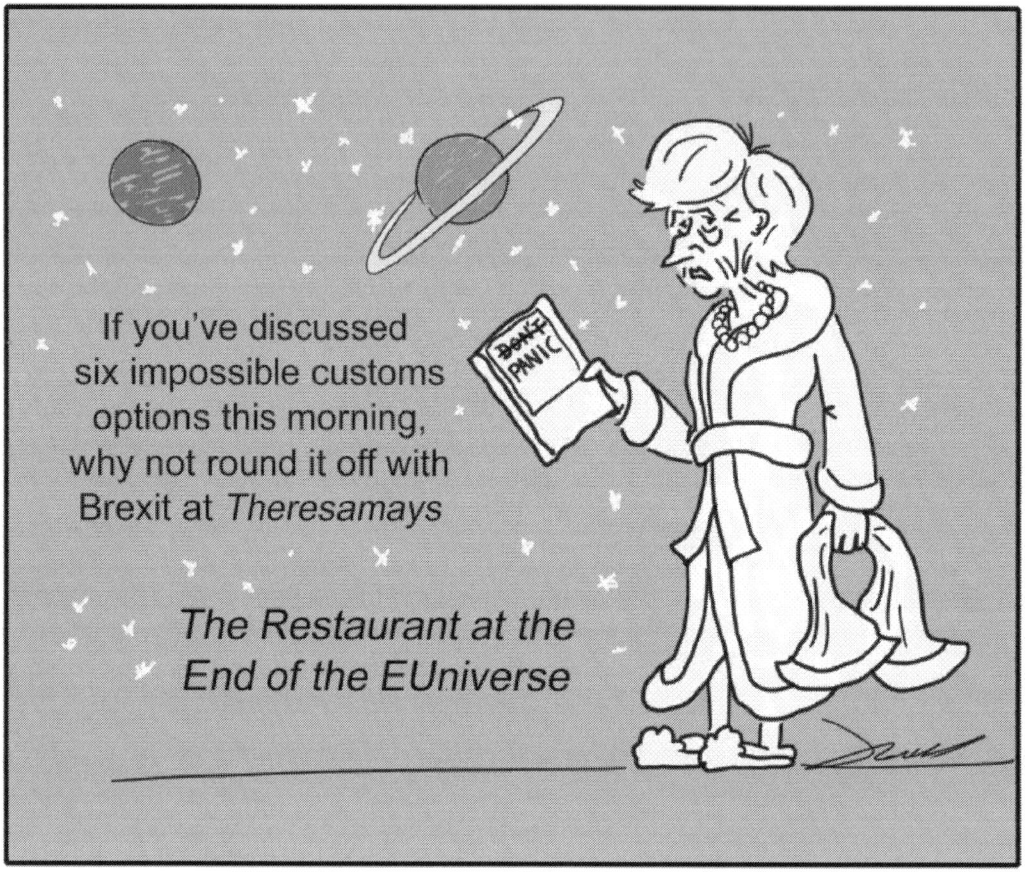
DON'T PANIC
If you've discussed
six impossible customs
options this morning,
why not round it off with
Brexit at *Theresamays*
The Restaurant at the
End of the EUniverse

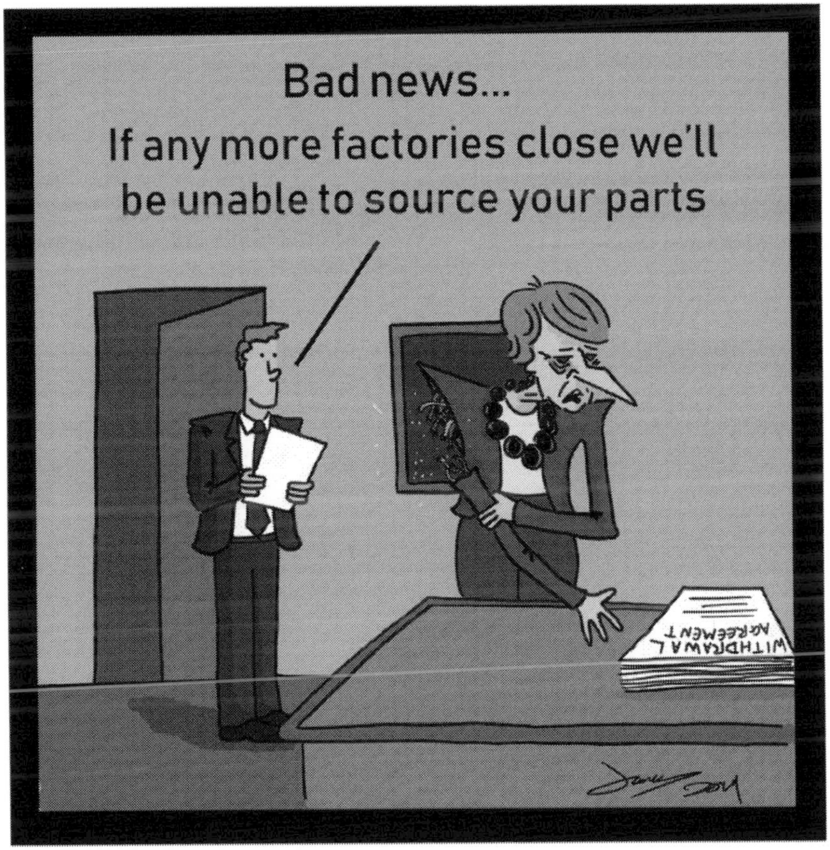
Bad news...
If any more factories close we'll be unable to source your parts
WITHDRAWAL AGREEMENT

A Game of Thrones

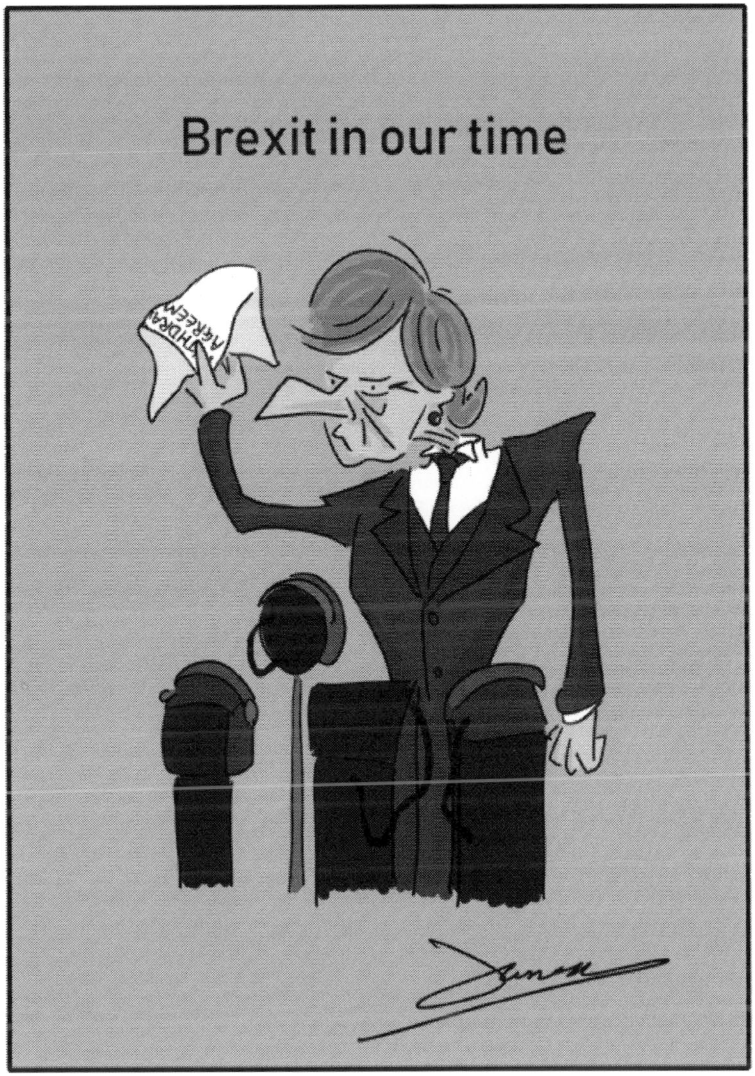
Brexit in our time

Maypole

European stage invasion

(Eurovision 2018)

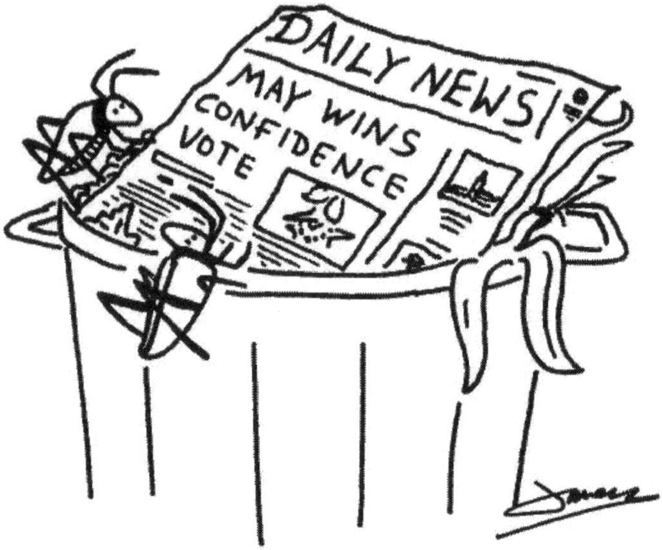
DAILY NEWS
MAY WINS CONFIDENCE VOTE

They say that in the event of nuclear war she'll be the only living thing to survive alongside us

I deeply regret not delivering Brexit, losing my majority, and standing on the Downing Street cat just before making this speech.

What Happened Next?

Don't you love farce?
My fault, I fear
I thought that you'd want what I want
Sorry, my dear!
But where are the clowns
Send in the clowns
Don't bother, they're here

Judy Collins, 1975

Tory Leadership: Runners and Riders

Boris Johnston
4/1

Statue of Thatcher
25/1

Pting
12/1

Michael 'Gover' Gove
7/2

Maybot 2.0
3.14259/1

Jacob Rees-Mogg
33/1

Dr Schnabel
40/1

Dominic Raab
adequate odds

jamesmellorcreative.com

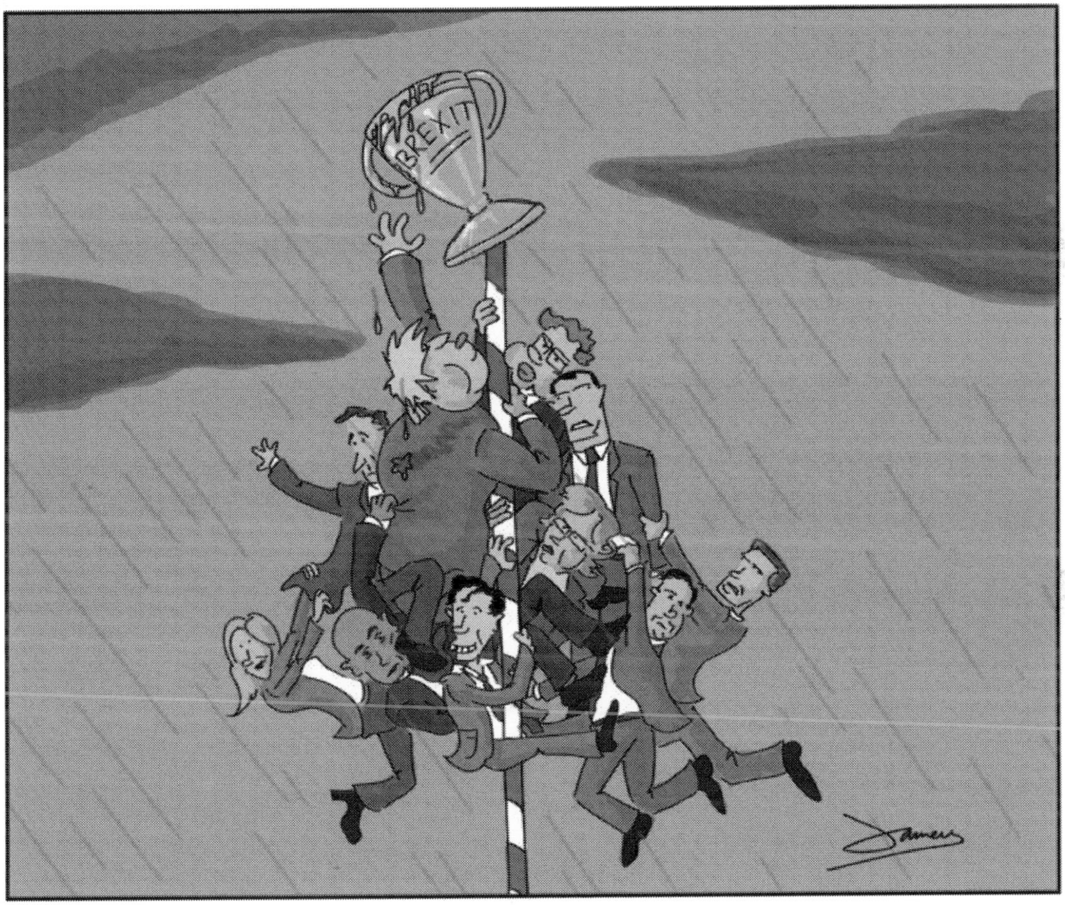
BREXIT

Really enjoyed my walk in Volcano Lair today
– wonderful and unexpected encounters with
henchmen wanting to discuss the theft of
spacecraft and provoking nuclear war.

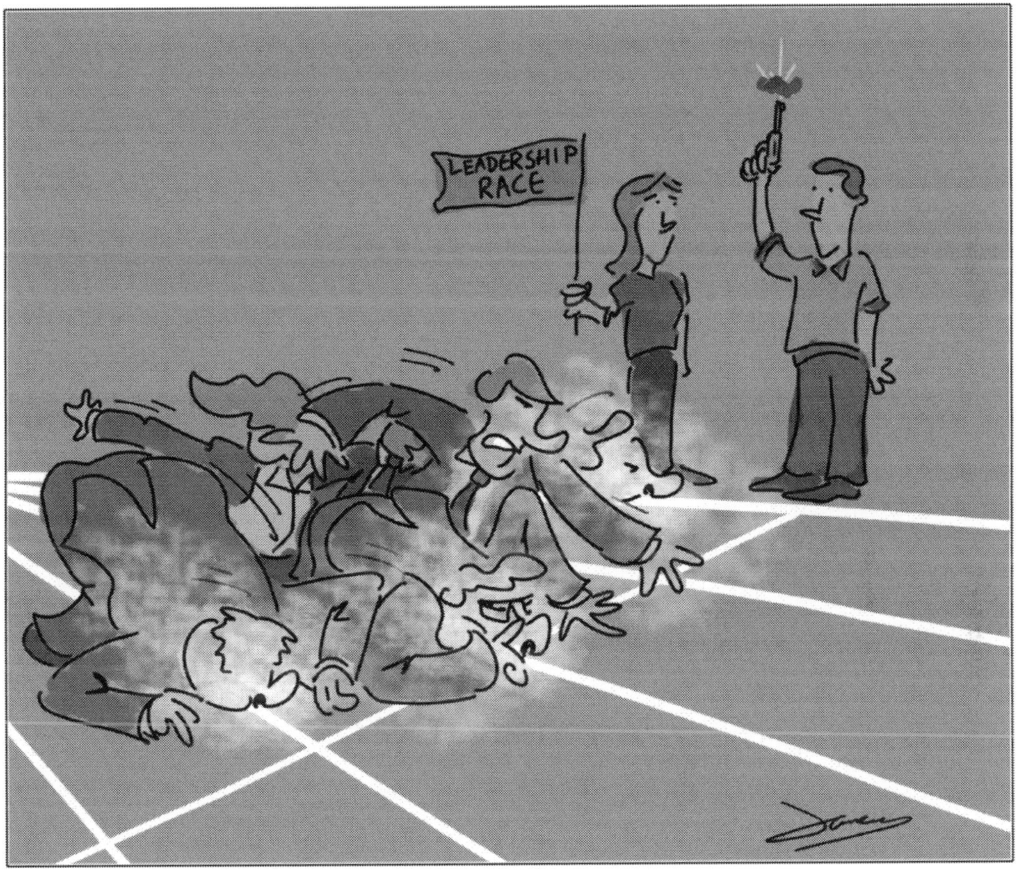
LEADERSHIP RACE

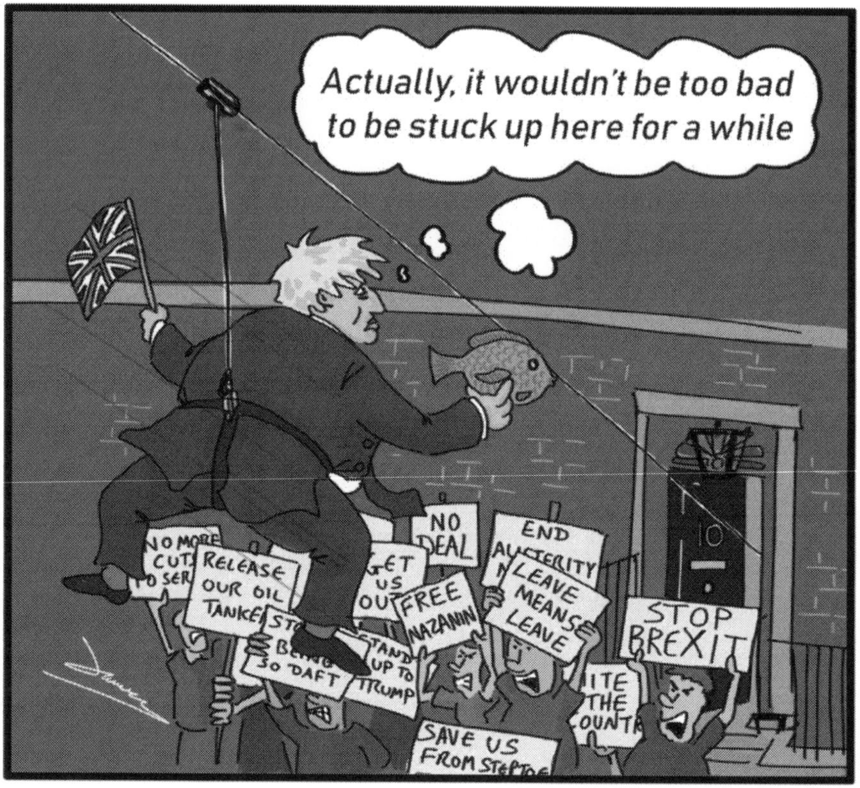

Actually, it wouldn't be too bad to be stuck up here for a while
NO DEAL
END AUSTERITY
GET US OUT
FREE NAZANIN
LEAVE MEANS LEAVE
STOP BREXIT
STAND UP TO TRUMP
SAVE US FROM STEPTOE
10

New PM arrives to face multiple crises

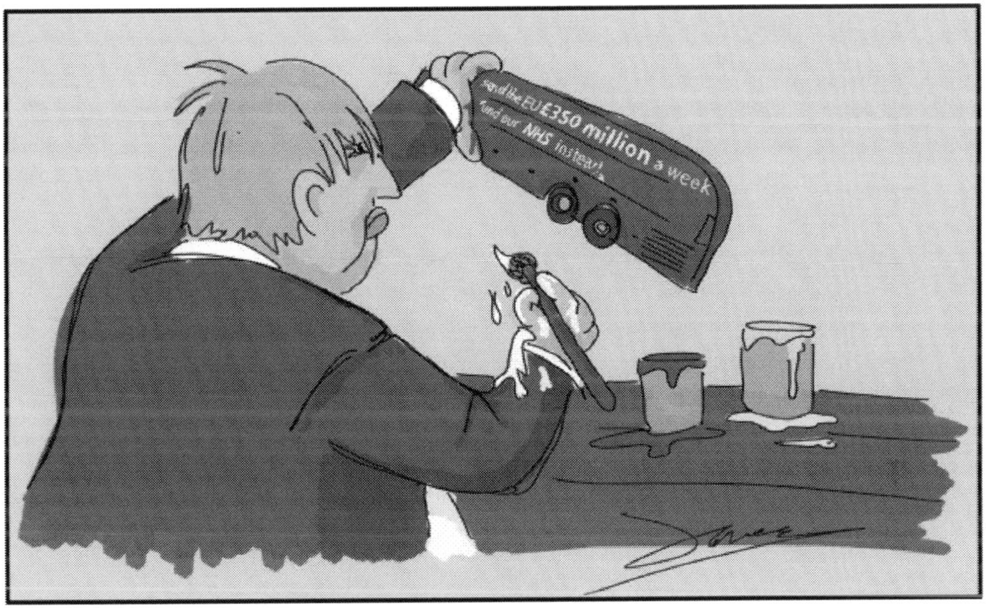
EU £350 million a week
fund our NHS instead

"I like to... paint. Or I make things. I make models of buses."

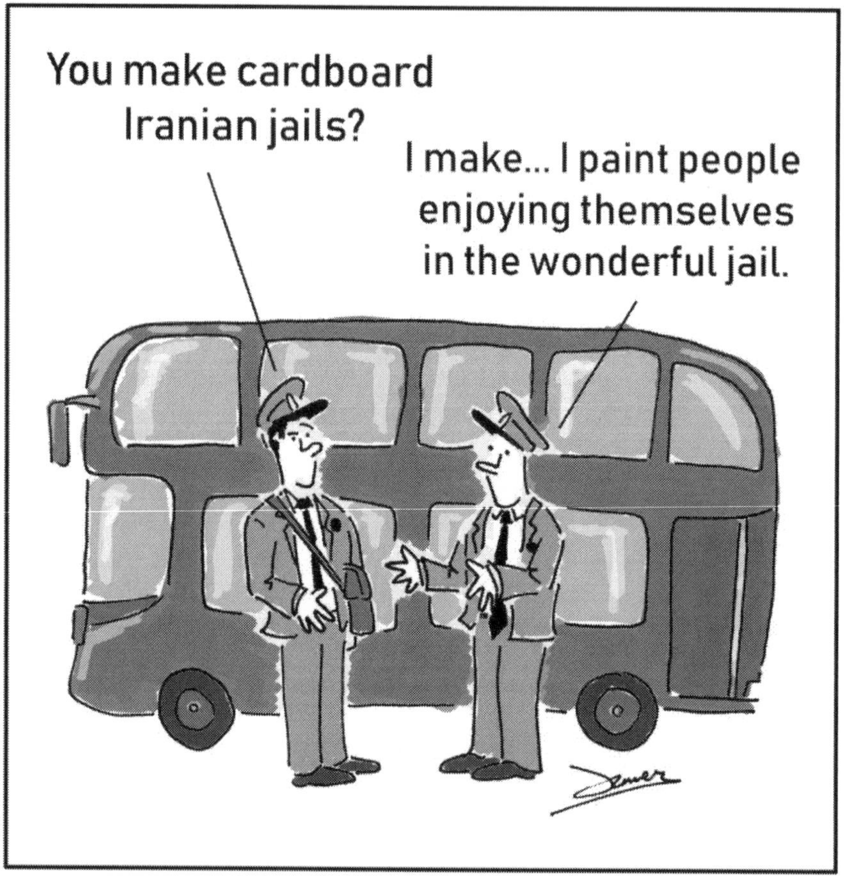
You make cardboard Iranian jails?
I make... I paint people enjoying themselves in the wonderful jail.

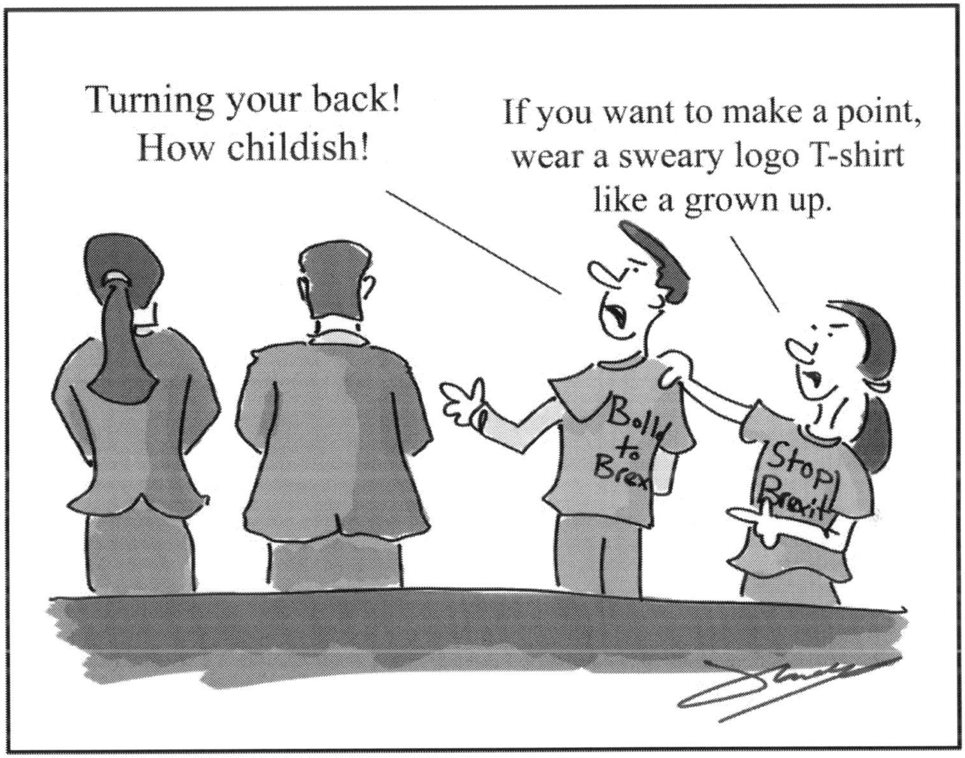
Turning your back!
How childish!
If you want to make a point,
wear a sweary logo T-shirt
like a grown up.

Brexit Party MEPs turn their backs to the EU anthem

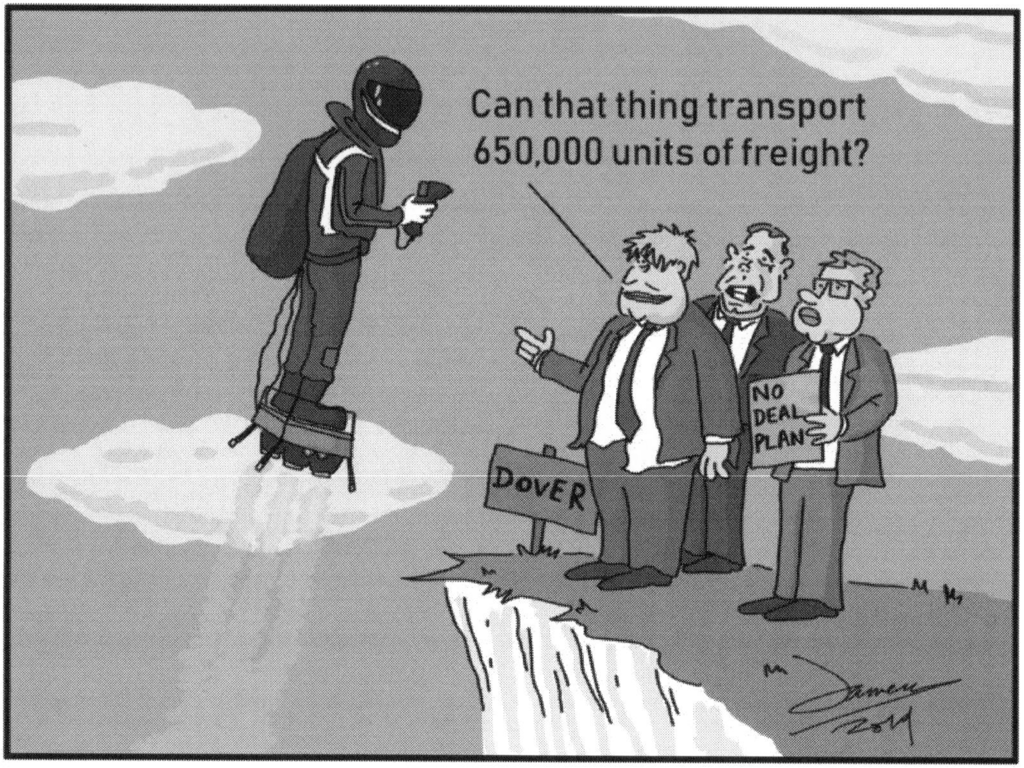
Can that thing transport
650,000 units of freight?
DOVER
NO DEAL PLAN

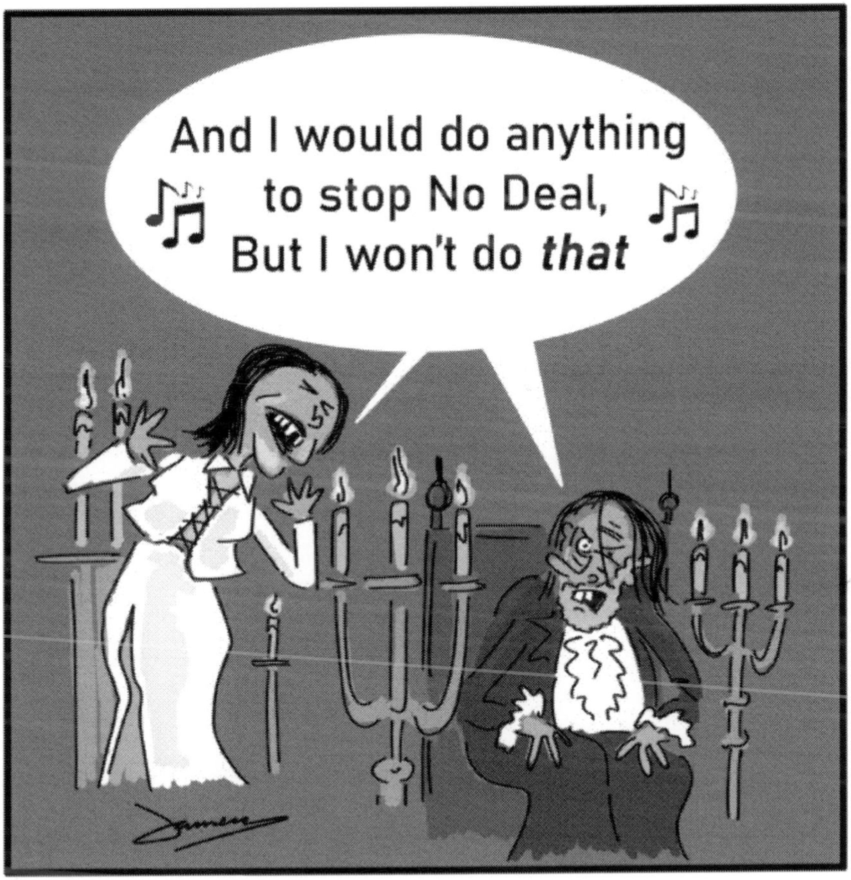
And I would do anything
to stop No Deal,
But I won't do *that*

Brexit, pursued by a Bear

Well, here we are. At the time of writing, absolutely none the wiser as to what's actually going to happen. A Deal, No Deal, or even no Brexit are still all in the running; though No Deal is a favourite seeing as it's already been implicitly voted for in the triggering of Article 50 (something quite a few MPs tend/try to forget). At the time of reading, things may be very different.

As has happened before, I've an odd sock drawer full of Brexit cartoons that either have not been published but I really rather like, or have been published but don't cleanly fit into any of the preceding chapters. Chronology be damned – here's a whole extra chapter of cartoons for you which I hope provide you with some therapeutic benefit.

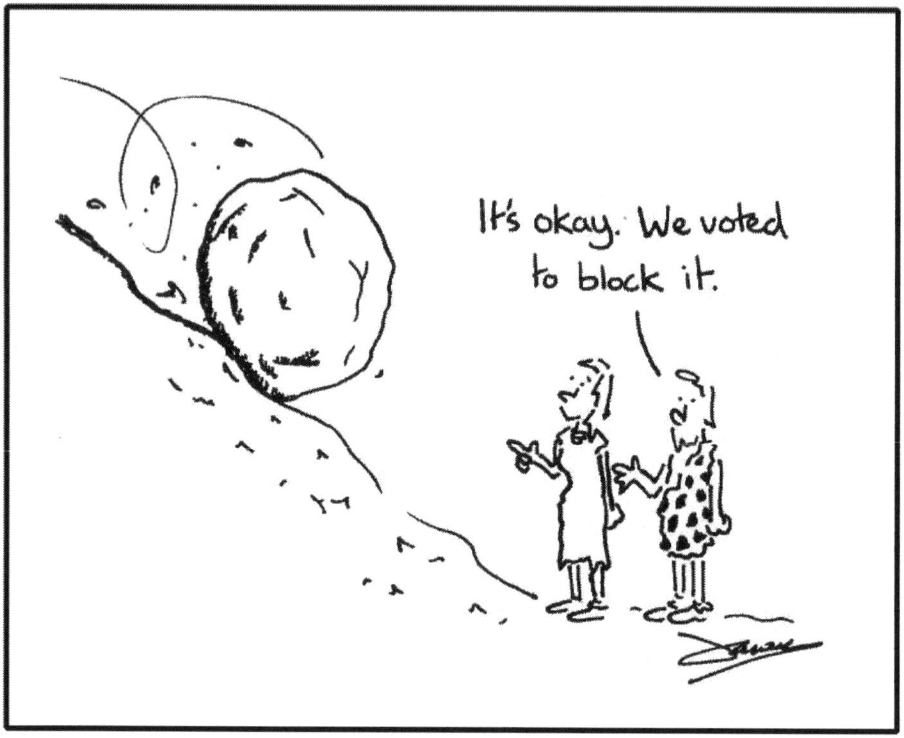
It's okay. We voted to block it.

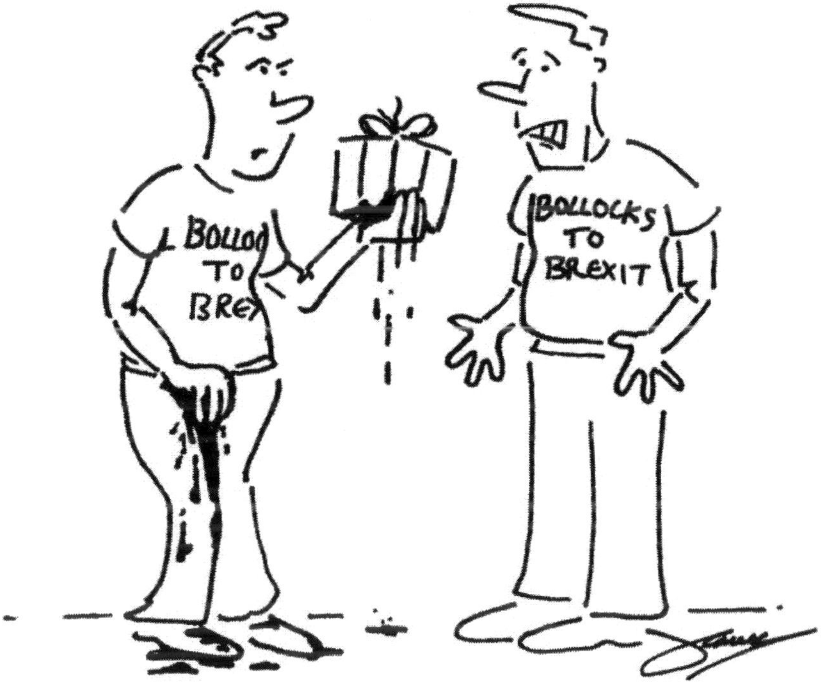
BOLLOCKS
TO
BREXIT

Where do I send them?

BREXIT
BREXIT EXTENSION
PEOPLES VOTE
(another spin)
you're a better shot than me
REVOKE ARTICLE 50

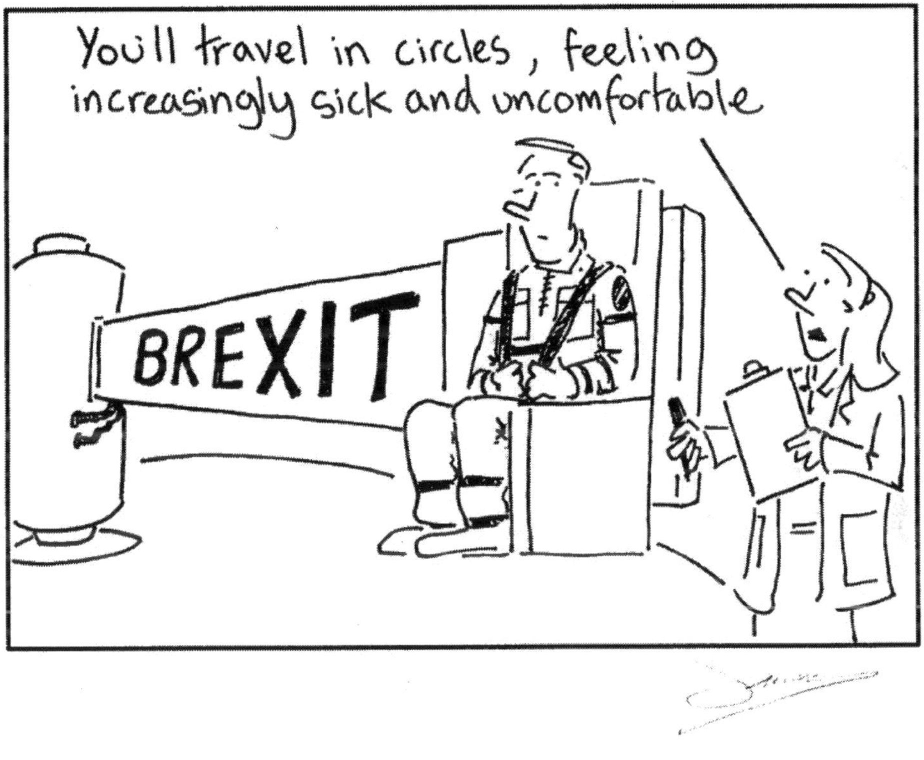
You'll travel in circles, feeling increasingly sick and uncomfortable
BREXIT

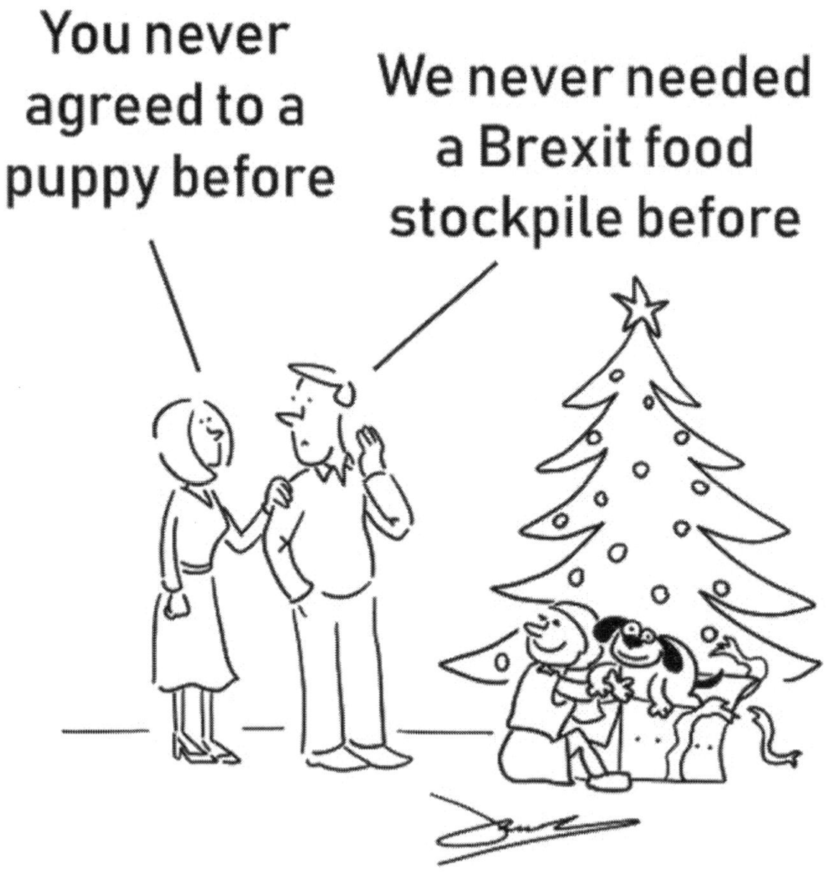
You never agreed to a puppy before
We never needed a Brexit food stockpile before

CROSS PARTY TALKS

VERY CROSS PARTY TALKS

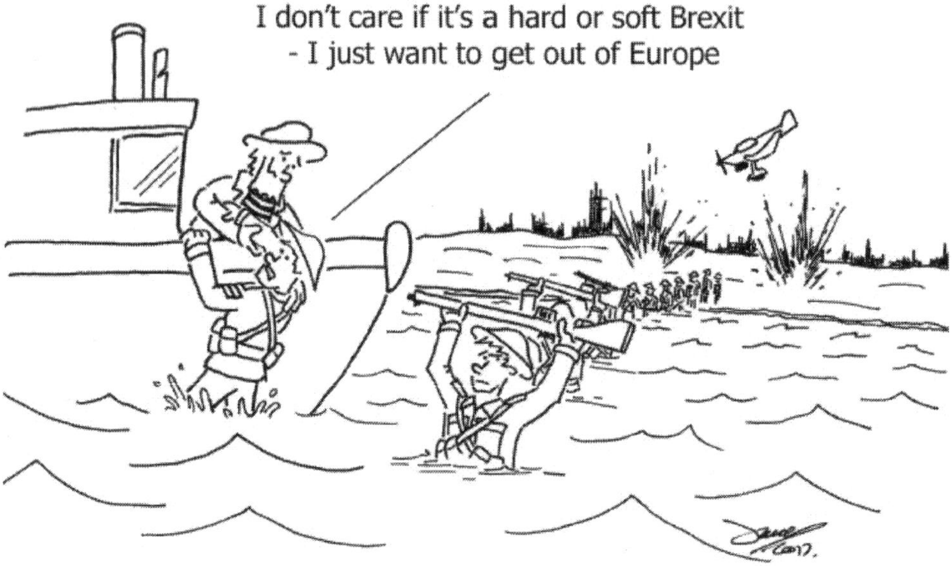
I don't care if it's a hard or soft Brexit
- I just want to get out of Europe

Dunkirk 1940

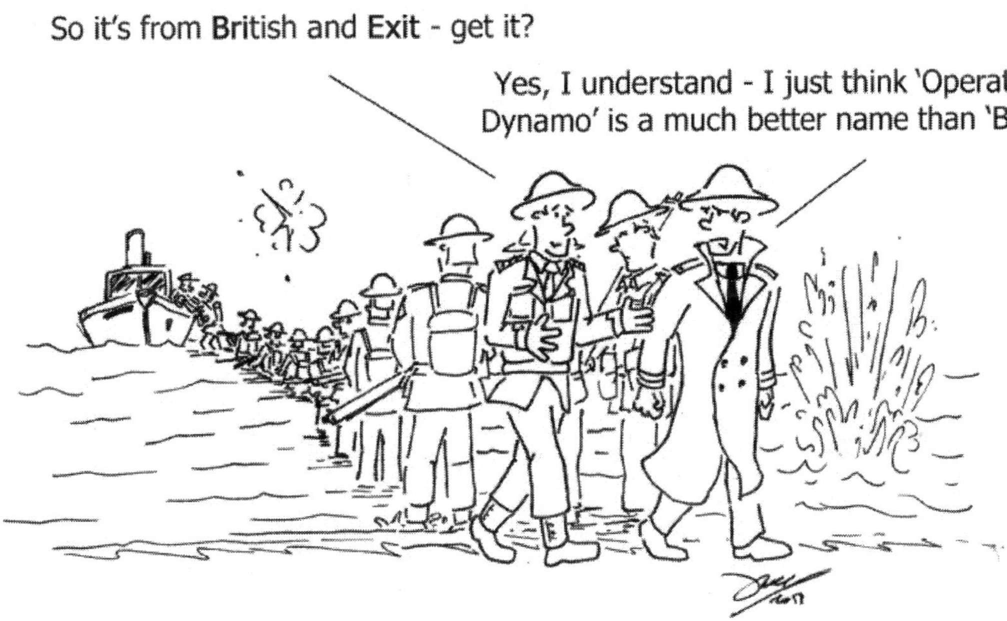
So it's from **Brit**ish and **Exit** - get it?
Yes, I understand - I just think 'Operation Dynamo' is a much better name than 'Brexit'

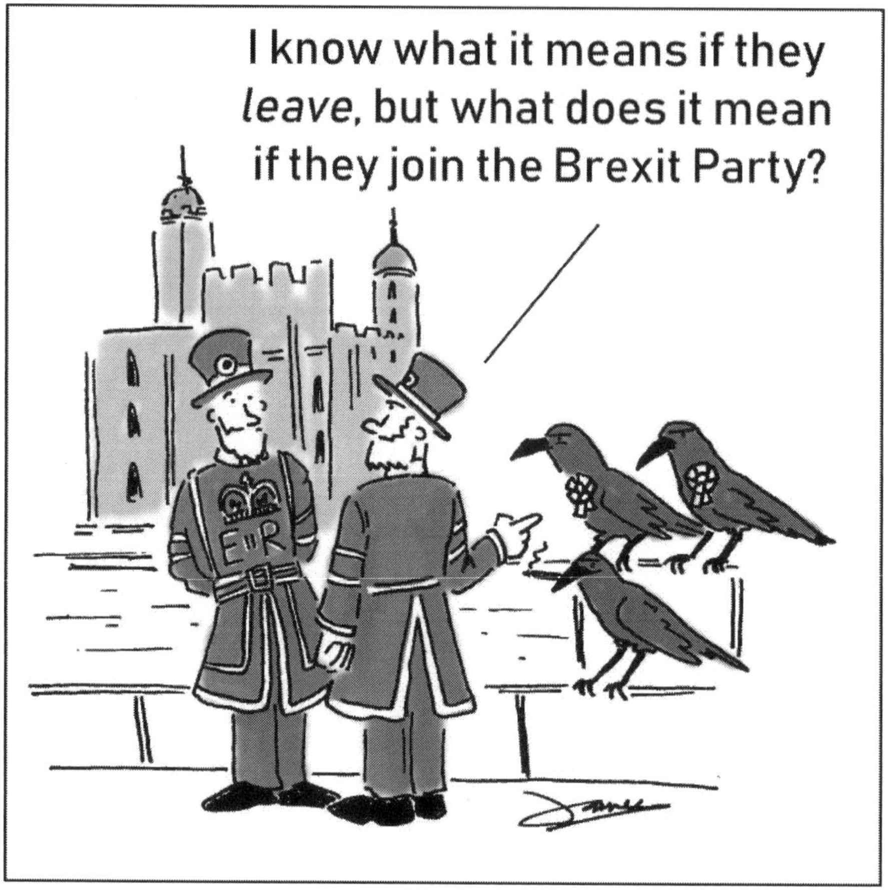
I know what it means if they *leave*, but what does it mean if they join the Brexit Party?

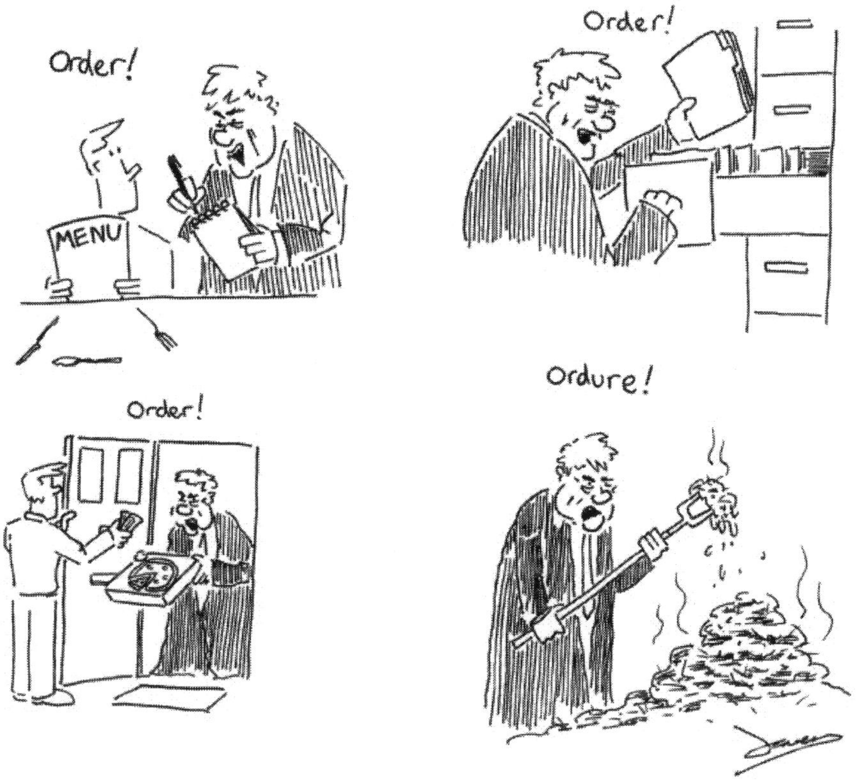
Order!
MENU
Order!
Order!
Ordure!

Alternative careers for a Speaker

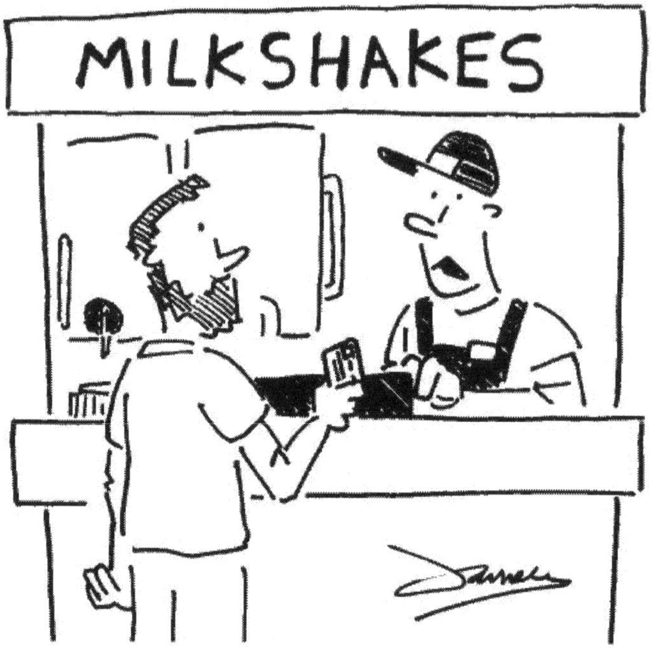
MILKSHAKES

To drink in, take away, or throw?

Groundhogs are half price
with every dead horse

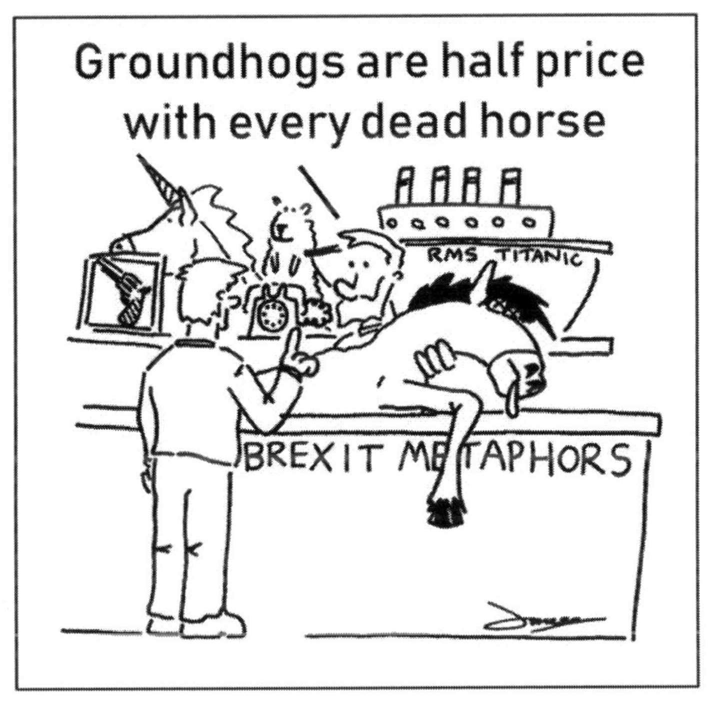
RMS TITANIC
BREXIT METAPHORS

Chapter 10

To be ~~continued~~ ~~concluded~~ continued...